Dare...
to Have Sex Everywhere but in Bed

Other titles in the Positively Sexual series

Dare… to Have Anal Sex by Coralie Trinh Thi

Dare… to Have Sex Everywhere but in Bed by Marc Dannam

Dare… to Make Love with 2, 3, 4…or More by Marc Dannam

Dare… to Try Bisexuality by Pierre des Esseintes

Dare… to Try Bondage by Axterdam

Dare… to Try Kama Sutra by Marc Dannam and Axterdam

Ordering
Trade bookstores in the U.S. and Canada please contact:

Publishers Group West
1700 Fourth Street, Berkeley CA 94710
Phone: (800) 788-3123   Fax: (800) 351-5073

Hunter House books are available at bulk discounts for textbook course adoptions; to qualifying community, health-care, and government organizations; and for special promotions and fund-raising. For details please contact:

Special Sales Department
Hunter House Inc., PO Box 2914, Alameda CA 94501-0914
Phone: (510) 865-5282   Fax: (510) 865-4295
E-mail: ordering@hunterhouse.com

Individuals can order our books from most bookstores,
by calling **(800) 266-5592**, or from our website at
www.hunterhouse.com

Marc Dannam

Dare...
to Have Sex Everywhere but in Bed

Osez… faire l'amour partout sauf dans un lit © La Musardine, France, 2004
Translation © 2009 Hunter House Publishers, Alameda, CA

All rights reserved. No part of this publication may be reproduced or transmitted in any form or by any means, electronic or mechanical, including photocopying and recording, or introduced into any information storage and retrieval system without the written permission of the copyright owner and the publisher of this book. Brief quotations may be used in reviews prepared for inclusion in a magazine, newspaper, or for broadcast. For further information please contact:

Hunter House Inc., Publishers
PO Box 2914
Alameda CA 94501-0914

Library of Congress Cataloging-in-Publication Data

Dannam, Marc.
  [Osez faire l'amour partout sauf dans un lit. English]
  Dare to have sex everywhere but in bed / Marc Dannam. — 1st ed.
      p. cm. — (Positively sexual series)
  "Osez faire l'amour partout sauf dans un lit."
  Includes index.
  ISBN 978-0-89793-513-5 (pbk.)
  1. Sex. I. Title.

HQ31.D224 2009
306.77—dc22   2009012543

Project Credits

Cover: Brian Dittmar Graphic Design	Editor: Alexandra Mummery
Cover Illustrator: Arthur de Pins	Publicity Associate: Sean Harvey
Book Production: John McKercher	Order Fulfillment: Washul Lakdhon
Copy Editor: Amy Bauman	Administrator: Theresa Nelson
Proofreader: John David Marion	Computer Support: Peter Eichelberger

Senior Marketing Associate: Reina Santana
Rights Coordinator: Candace Groskreutz
Customer Service Manager: Christina Sverdrup
Publisher: Kiran S. Rana

Printed and Bound by Bang Printing

Manufactured in the United States of America

9 8 7 6 5 4 3 2 1   First Edition   09 10 11 12 13

Contents

Foreword to the U.S. Edition
by Yvonne K. Fulbright, PhD vii

Prologue 1
   A Solemn Warning and Friendly Advice 2

1 In Your Bed, Nevertheless… 3
   Change the Décor 3
   Dress Up 4
   Use Your Imagination 5
   Change the Bed 16

2 At the House 19
   Around Your Apartment 19
   All the Other Rooms of the House 24
   The Furniture 35

3 At Work 43
   At the Office 43
   Business 48
   A Few Special Professions 49

4 In Town 51
   Out in the Open! 51

Wedged Between a Few Walls...but Well out of Sight! ... 54

5 Evening Parties ... 62
In a Restaurant ... 62
At the Movies ... 63
In a (Dance) Club ... 64

6 On Vacation ... 71
Ground Transportation ... 71
On the Water ... 79
Public Transportation ... 81

7 In the Countryside ... 86
L'Amour Outdoor ... 86
A Trip to the Woods ... 88
Some Rural Areas to Do It ... 94
In the Forest ... 95

8 At the Beach or in the Mountains ... 100
At the Seaside ... 100
On Vacation ... 108
In the Mountains ... 114

Bibliography ... 117

Note: Some books quoted in this work have English-language editions; our text is translated from the French original and may not match the exact wording of the published English text.

Foreword to the U.S. Edition

by Yvonne K. Fulbright, PhD

◉ ...the Series

Leave it to the superbly sensual French to make the exotic all the more erotic, enticing, and accessible with the most charming set of sex books ever released.

When I first saw the *Osez...* (Dare) series, I was instantly seduced by the playful, titillating covers of this set of more than twenty pocket books. Delightfully disarming, these works inspire one to take on all taboos, summoning lovers to unleash their sexual nature as never before. Talk about *ooo-là-là*—these books leave no doubt as to why the French are known the world over for being sexy. Whether it is their food, wine, fashion, or simply their sensual language, the French are credited and revered for encouraging eroticism.

Throw the word *French* in front of any English word(s)—whether it is French underwear, French maid outfit, French kiss, or French champagne—and

> **He cracks the code for doing the unthinkable and, in many cases, the illegal...**

it is suddenly sexy. This book is no exception. Translated into Portuguese, Spanish, and Italian, this book is now available in English for your delight. In charming lovers to "carpe diem," it urges them to seek their pleasure as never before.

◉ ...this Book

People have long enjoyed hinting at their trysts beyond the boudoir. Some even openly brag that they've "been there; done that" when it comes to the many places where people pursue passion. Believe me, as a sexologist, sex educator, and columnist, I know. I couldn't believe the positive feedback a column I wrote for Foxnews.com received on this matter. While I noted a number of the many locales where lovers have been known to get busy, a few e-mails enthusiastically mentioned even more. Given the popularity of sex anywhere, a collection of places of carnal hanky-panky has been long overdue.

Enter Marc Dannam, your French tour guide to getting it on in places you've likely never considered, or at least never dared to try. This author, one of sixteen scribes behind the original French *Osez…* (Dare) series, equips lovers with the most thorough and well-thought-out list of places to express your amour. From revamping your love nest to christening every room in the house to delving into the world beyond your front door, in the great outdoors, while shopping, traveling, or discovering a city escape, Dannam seductively dares lovers of all orientations to attempt the traditional and unconventional.

This book challenges you to use your imagination, especially as opportunities present themselves. Dannam dishes out everything you need to know to create breathless action, helping you to enhance these special experiences. Readers are given tips for guaranteeing physical comfort and how to sex things up even further. The most timid and wary are given emotional reassurances, complemented by quotes and lovers' stories, with Dannam's only shortcoming being in his inability to act as a beyond-the-chateau lookout.

Instead, the author provides lovers with everything they need to know about sex outside of the bedroom. He outlines the difficulties in attempting sex in each location, the preparation needed, potential costs, the reward for your efforts, the degree of risk, and any inconveniences such sexy situations pose. He cracks the code for doing the unthinkable and, in many cases, the illegal (which invites what goes without saying: Pursue at your own risk). This is the closest thing you'll get to an intimate, interactive tour on this topic, and this muse will have you guessing: What will he think of next? Perhaps the better question is: What will inspired lovers think of next?

So without further ado, let's take a look at all of the places in which adventurous lovers have dared to have sex.

— Yvonne K. Fulbright, PhD, MSEd
Professor of Human Sexuality, Argosy University
Coauthor, *Your Orgasmic Pregnancy*
Author of *The Hot Guide to Safer Sex* and *Touch Me There!*

Important Note

The material in this book is intended to provide a review of information regarding sexual play. Every effort has been made to provide accurate and dependable information. We believe that the sensuality advice given in this book poses no risk to any healthy person. However, if you have any sexually transmitted diseases, we recommend consulting your doctor before using any of the ideas presented in this book.

The publisher, authors, and editors, as well as the professionals quoted in the book, cannot be held responsible for any error, omission, professional disagreement, or dated material, and are not liable for any damage, injury, or other adverse outcome of applying any of the information resources in this book. If you have questions concerning the application of the information described in this book, consult a qualified professional.

Prologue

> **"I love what is forbidden, rude pleasures…"**
> — *"Maman a tort"* (Mommy Is Wrong), song interpreted by Mylene Farmer, words by Jerome Dahan

The vast majority of sexual encounters occur in a bed, the conjugal bed most often, sometimes in a hotel room or a meeting place, but in a bed. Admittedly, a large bed is very convenient and is perfect for sexual activities, particularly with clean sheets, all fresh and soft, and a nice mattress that fits the curves of the bodies of the two partners who find themselves upon it and offers just enough spring so that each thrust is followed by a delicious rebound.

A bed is surely the best.

But the world is big, and your bedroom is small. Dare to go out! Dare to leave your comfy bed where you have already enjoyed a significant amount of frolicking. Dare to visit other rooms, to use other furnishings, to try out the many possibilities offered by public places, transportation, your building.… Go out into nature; go make love in the sea or a river, on the beach, among the dunes, in the woods, in the hay, in the mountains, and—why not?—in the snow.

Dare to consider it; we'll tell you how to accomplish it.

◎ A Solemn Warning and Friendly Advice

Caution: Do not forget the legal risks. It is best to know what laws your adventures could break. It could cost you a fine or worse!

So be realistic! What follows is not an invitation to get yourself into trouble; consider yourself warned that much of what follows could be risky, depending on where you live. All the same—and at the very least—you will find a few juicy stories to ignite or enrich your fantasies.

THE COST OF LOVE The ideas and examples in this book are presented in a very practical form. Each one of the scenarios includes comments based upon six principal criteria:

DIFFICULTY: How hard it is to make the scenario happen.

PREPARATION: From just a few seconds (the time it takes to decide) to several hours (the time it takes to set the décor or create an ideal situation).

COST: How much money you'll need to make an adventure happen.

PLEASURE: The level of pleasure this adventure can bring to its participants. (Obviously, this is a very subjective criterion.)

RISK: Any real danger, penalties, or legal issues that this adventure may invite.

INCONVENIENCES: Embarrassments, problem areas, and matters that may be less serious but should not be ignored.

STRAIGHT OR GAY This guide does not differentiate between same-sex and heterosexual liaisons. Nevertheless, for our purposes, the two partners will be referred to as *he* and *she*. We suggest our gay friends interpret this as "active and passive" or "me and my friend," or whatever feels best.

ch 1. In Your Bed, Nevertheless...

The place everything in this book starts, from where we will take off for a thousand frolics, is your bedroom and your bed. In order to make this work, we have to make something special out of your ordinary, everyday bed so that your bedroom doesn't seem like your bedroom. Instead it should feel like an exotic chamber in which you can imagine yourself somewhere else, without being reminded that this is the place where you doze off every night.

◎ Change the Décor Before launching on this grand adventure, we have to gather some supplies. We suggest this now in the hope that you won't need to go grocery shopping or to a department store once you begin working on your great escapes "wish list."

SUITCASE OF TREASURES Ideally, you will always have the following types of supplies close by:

- Attractive bed linens. Pure white or solid colors in reds and blacks are great for big occasions. These evoke a level of sensuality different from stuffed toys and a patchwork quilt

unless, of course, your idea of a fantasy takes place in the 1970s, in which case a quilt would be perfect....
- A futon-type mattress may be useful for rolling around on the floor in rooms other than the bedroom or if you want to be out on the balcony.
- Mirrors of every size. Have at least one mirror at the foot of the bed and others on the walls or mounted on the furniture or ceilings so that you can watch yourselves as you assume positions on your bed or couch.
- Drapes, screens, fabrics, mosquito nets, cover-ups. You can use all of these things to modify the space in your bedroom and other rooms.
- Many pillows.
- Perfumes, massage oils, and incense.
- Candelabras (candleholders), scented candles, soft-light lamps, spotlights.
- X-rated movies, sexy magazines, a small library of "curiosities" and erotic literature.

As an afternoon or evening of fooling around requires you to be clean and fresh, made-up, and groomed, it is a good idea to have plenty of bubble bath, beauty products, washcloths, and towels.

◉ Dress Up

THE PERFECT OUTFIT To create a wardrobe suitable for amorous encounters, you should include the following types of items:

- Makeup, feathers, costume jewelry, various disguises, Halloween or Mardi Gras costumes, ribbons and fabrics, etc.

- Lingerie or provocative underwear for the ladies. Go for as skimpy as possible, with strings that can be untied or torn off! A pleated skirt for when you are rambling about; two or three bustiers; one or two garter belts; one or two pairs of thongs, panties, and stockings; transparent nighties; and at least one very cheesy, slutty outfit, with pink fur, etc. Men should possess similarly appropriate underwear and accoutrements.
- Leather clothes, skirts, pants, T-shirts, a leather or latex collar, combinations with vinyl….
- Masks, blindfolds, scarves, handcuffs, condoms/contraceptives/protection, and a cock ring. Don't forget your favorite sex toys.

Use Your Imagination But wait, let me tell you a little something else.

PILLOW (TALK) HANDBOOK Geishas have collections of erotic drawings and instructions on how to spark flames in their lovers. These works are known as Pillow Books. Casanova had a volume of figure drawings by l'Aretin. This collection of sketches contained thirty-five sexual poses. Casanova referenced them often. In 1772, he met a pretty Jewish girl, Lia, whom he tried to excite by showing her several drawings from this naughty book. The young lady forced herself to ask very embarrassing questions to which Casanova smugly responded, "Allow us to know the gestures as well as the words. It is better that way."

Why wouldn't you want to have one of these books? Or, if not a "reference book," you could create your own album of sorts. This album could be a collection of the words and images that turn you on, stashed away in a drawer not far from your bed or other hideaways around the house? Only one? Or two even? The album itself will be a dreamland you can share. Each time you are provoked by an enticing image or work of pornography, clip it out and save it, arrange it, and classify it. Your album—packed with invitations to swinger parties, advertisements for XXX movies, and explicit postcards—from old figure drawings of nudes posing sensually to the raunchiest smut—will be a collection of the images that excite your lust. When you feel yourself getting into the mood, you can flip through it together.

The rest is up to you.

You and your partner could just as well have separate albums that you fill with the images that provoke your own desires. You could then find a thousand uses for them. Looking at each other's album might become a way to send messages to your partner. You can show him/her an image that particularly excites you, revealing a position or a situation you want to experience.

SOME SUGGESTIONS Fully supplied, your house and your bed can be transformed into a theater for the realization of multiple fantasies. You can take turns creating the magic, either deciding together what you want or allowing for pleasant surprises from one another. In a very short time, you could change your outlook on your sex life and wind up doing somersaults and jumping for joy. The potential effects are immense.

Presented below are some basic ideas and scenarios. It is up to you to take these suggestions further.

≈ *Ambience: Empire of the Senses*

Let's be Japanese in our décor! A few things will suffice to completely change the atmosphere of your room. It is easy: First, push everything to one side or into another room! In fact, the more furniture you can move into another room, the more your bedroom becomes "Zen-enlightened." A folding screen made of rice paper is perfect to block off a space where a few paper lantern shades and a futon mattress on the floor can help you to create a completely different ambience.

Shopping

Your day will be dedicated to a long promenade through the Asian stores and the sex shops of your city. In a sex shop, you'll want to shop for a dildo; it should be small in diameter and made of strong, stiff material. Try to find a cock ring large enough to encircle his genitals, too. But most importantly, you will want to purchase a lovely pair of geisha balls. How long have you wanted those?

Geisha balls are hollow metal balls with marbles inside, sold by the pair. They are inserted into the vagina. When they start to vibrate, the movement they provide provokes amazing sensations. Originally, one of the two balls was gold, and the other was silver. As soon as the geisha balls are purchased, she should duck into a private spot and slide them inside her vagina. A restaurant bathroom will do. From this moment forward, she can expect a most agreeable afternoon.

You might then go into an Oriental clothing store where you can buy lightweight kimonos. She will try them on, naked in the changing room, with him slipping in to see her. She will be rewarded for being naughty.... Her sexual organs have been vibrating forever, it seems. She begins to have trouble controlling herself, each one of her movements increases the pleasure building from her innermost depths. He will surely know how to make the most of this situation.

Prelude

Return home to your dwelling, which has been set up like a Japanese temple. Each of you should dress in Asian clothing, and the new Japanese robes or kimonos will be both comfortable and enticing.

Try sushi or Japanese food for dinner, using ginger to create a stimulating, warming effect. Next, plan for a sensual bath or a soak in a hot tub. Either one will be the perfect next step after your Asian meal.

A few glasses of sake later, and the night can be dedicated to ancestral sexual practices. Costumed as you are—she nude under her silk, and he wearing cloth briefs like a judo master—you work it out in the shadows. First though, the geisha balls are removed from Madame. With a ribbon, she then binds her dildo to her ankle, against the heel, the tip turned away from the foot. She may thus imitate Japanese women using their *harigata*—a wooden probe—to pleasure themselves. With a slow movement of the leg, she brings the probe against the vulva and then caresses and penetrates herself. Monsieur pulls the cock ring over his penis, as did the Japanese men of the eighteenth century, to strengthen their erections with *zuikis*, rings for the penis of every sort that could give them just as much pleasure as their partners. Should you be so inclined, you could try bondage. A quality rope that is smooth and clean can have many additional uses. One of the Japanese erotic games, the rope game, was an erotic adaptation of a type of wrestling. The two partners would tie themselves together (by the wrist, for example) and would not untie the rope for the duration of the "assault." Making love in this way is not without risks—the risk of twisting yourselves into an embarrassing tangle in the cord.

After having made love, she wipes herself delicately and wipes him, using small shreds of tissue paper that are cast on the floor as a sign of satisfaction. The number of shreds on the floor indicates the intensity of her pleasure. Don't argue with tradition.

The night might go on in this way until the coming of the rising sun.

DIFFICULTY: None.

PREPARATION: A long day of shopping; moving some furniture around in the house.

COST: From $50 to $500 depending on the quality of the items and food you purchase.

PLEASURE: Subtle, medium hard, medium cerebral

RISKS: None.

INCONVENIENCES: Your date risks forgetting her geisha balls as she stumbles home the next day. Or, if she reinserts them, she risks having another orgasm in transit!

Recommended Viewing

Empire of the Senses by Nagisa Oshima. Directed by Nagisa Oshima. Argos Films, 1977.

Warning: This movie's final scenes depict strangulation and castration (which are included to deny the film its philosophical dimension!). Yet these scenes are well worth ignoring for the sake of some inspirational and aesthetically perfect images: games with food, the way the girls' kimonos are hiked up, and how nothing is put on for the boys.... The more adventurous among you will attempt to get a few recent pornographic productions and discover the dreamy bodies of Fujiko Kano or Mimi Miyagi.

Recommended Reading

Japanese pillow books, for sale in some sex shops and bookstores. Check out *Shunga: The Essence of Japanese Pillow-Book Eroticism* (Norton), *Gardens of Pleasure: Eroticism and Art in China* (Norton), and *The Complete Illustrated Kama Sutra* (Dane). Collections of Japanese prints, particularly by the famous *Ukiyo-e*.

≈ *Ambience: Total Blackout*

This scenario involves an atmosphere that is black as night; complete darkness for the whole weekend.

With respect to the definition of love, the German physicist and writer Christoph Georg Lichtenberg says, "There are very few things of which we can acquire a conception through all five senses."

And from the Roman poet Ovid, "Generally, we use a sheet to cover up everything that is indecent to reveal, or we otherwise keep it to the shadows, at least half-obscured."

A number of women prefer to make love in the dark. In explanation, they offer a variety of reasons: They don't like the idea of their partner seeing them naked. According to them, their body has imperfections that are better hidden from view—made even more complicated by issues like modesty and worry about being surprised by the kids.

But in our book, this is not the reason why we turn out the lights. The deprivation of one of the senses—sight—seems to have the effect of intensifying the others. Making love in the dark is a practice that has fallen off the map, regarded as "old-fashioned" by younger generations. So this is the perfect time to revive it, radically. Let's live and (make) love in total darkness for two days—or a little less time if you must.

Decorations

One of the two partners temporarily rearranges the apartment, and specifically the bedroom, moving furniture around and changing the placement of several objects. The most important thing is to store things that can hurt someone or may become dangerous in the dark. Block out all of the windows with dark curtains or black construction paper, take out most of the light bulbs, and leave no light except in the bathroom (candles) and maybe in the kitchen. You will need a good supply of heavy cloth to block out even the faintest light. The rooms reserved for your frolicking should be plunged into total darkness.

Costume

Don't worry about your clothes. What is important is that both partners ignore how the other is dressed. Since taking each other's clothes off will be part of the fun, wearing complicated or unfamiliar clothes becomes a kind of guilty pleasure. You can even change clothes secretly to add to the games. Even mealtime around the kitchen table—sacred ground!—is a good place to grab each other and try to guess what the other is wearing.

Games and Foreplay

First, try hide-and-go-seek. Next, Marco-Polo! And for the finale, "How close can we get?"—and that's about all you need for the weekend. Anything goes, including pleasant surprises and romantic gestures. It is an opportune time to introduce a new toy that both of you can enjoy, name your new cock ring, or wear something new where you know it will be found and fondled....

DIFFICULTY: Depends on the scenario and your tastes.
PREPARATION: Time consuming, but well worth the effort.
COST: Negligible unless you have to replace something you crash into.
PLEASURE: Unique; nearly perfect.
RISKS: Real danger of serious injury? None.
INCONVENIENCES: Bruises, a broken vase, banged-up knees from furniture. The only real loss is not to be able to see your partner's gorgeousness!

≈ *Ambience: Pretend to Be a Porn Star*

The actors and starlets exaggerate lovemaking so that it both does and doesn't look "fake": They get it on; the men ejaculate. The facial expressions are exaggerated for each movement and become part of the show, like the moans, the eyes rolling back, the gobs of goo spattered on the screen.

We are going to play along; it is a small stretch of the imagination.

The Set

Two choices present themselves in this adventure. In the first version, you can use a video camera so that you can film your frolicking. In the second version, the camera is replaced by a series of mirrors for a less long-term impact.

In addition to cameras and mirrors, you simply must have a video player and several imposing X-rated titles. You have two days and a long night ahead of you—so try to be prepared! And ready yourself to copy all of the action, scene for scene, and become the actors in these lovely films. Don't forget to ham it up and play the cheesy seduction.

Décor

Your bedroom—and especially your bed—will be extremely well lit with a series of spotlights throwing bright light everywhere. The camera, if you decide to use one, will be mounted on a tripod; mirrors will be situated so that they are horizontal and give the impression of watching a wide screen. Mirrors should be set up in other rooms as well, ready for use when you change the location of your romp. The TV should be placed on a cart or table that can be moved from room to room in order to keep the action with you.

Look

Porn stars and starlets are for the most part tanned and smooth. Hair removal from your private areas is the first chore for the day, which means you will have to buy shaving cream and a good razor. The best thing to do is shave a day or two in advance, so that skin irritation won't be a problem when things heat up. She can do her hair and makeup to look like a sitcom actress, wear high heeled shoes that she will almost never take off, add a chain around her hips, hoop earrings, and a tattoo below the waistline (a temporary one will do nicely). Whatever little she may be wearing, she should have garters, with white frills and a robe that is easy to toss aside. In this scenario, being racy is part of the act.

Behind the Cameras

A very hot weekend—an X-rated one—begins with a visit to the best-stocked video/sex shop in town. Ideally, you will have all sorts of videos to choose from: recent releases from your favorite porn producer; American/Euro porn; classics from the 1970s; or other productions generally referred to as compilations (or multiscene productions). If you are looking for videos that might appeal to women because they have more plot, costumes, etc., consider looking for videos produced by Candida Royalle.

As your head swims with juicy images, you can rush home for this special weekend—or get a limo if you prefer. You two are stars, after all. On the top or on the bottom, seductress or seduced…choose from any scenario borrowed from the films or create your own. Really, there's nothing to it.

Scenario

Anna Span, author of the title *Erotic Home Videos*, suggests for her audience a list of ordinary roles assumed in the dominant/submissive genre of X-rated film scenarios. Here then, from an excellent source, are several types of encounters that may inspire you:

- master/slave
- judge/criminal
- nurse/patient
- executive/chauffeur
- princess or prince/commoner
- boss/secretary
- professor/student
- rock star/groupie
- cop/thief
- doctor/patient

Sexual Practices

It is not the way you make love or the positions you achieve that is important—though you will prove to yourself that it is better to try all the positions—but what appears on screen or before the mirrors. It is important to be flexible and in shape, so that when you groan as you are about to get off, it is not because you are fatigued. The final scene culminates with the obvious ejaculation in full view. You are not obliged to copy the money shot unless you want to verify that semen irritates your eyes.

Note: Of course, as a result of the "normal" male ejaculatory reflex, most couples who don't have access to Viagra risk running out of steam (!) before Saturday afternoon.

DIFFICULTIES: Practically none.

PREPARATIONS: The most attention goes to the choice and placement of mirrors, or to the choice of camera and film equipment and setting it up. This information may be a little technical, but you can do it.

COST: Expense varies according to the equipment you buy.

PLEASURE: Narcissistic, voyeuristic, acrobatic, and hard-core.

RISKS: The greatest risk is that the tapes could get out and fall into the wrong hands: ex-lovers, spouses, tattletales, the maid, kids, reality TV producers, etc. Therefore, it is very important to keep all of your taped material under lock and key—unless it is part of your fantasy that a copy gets out. But even if leaking a tape is part of your fantasy experience, you have to assume that the tape will eventually wind up in the wrong hands.

INCONVENIENCES: Cramps more than anything, camera blindness, twisted neck from trying to see yourself. Nothing serious.

Recommended Reading

The Wise Woman's Guide to Erotic Videos by Angela Cohen and Sarah Fox. New York: Broadway Books, 1997.

The Ultimate Guide to Adult Video by Violet Blue. San Francisco, CA: Cleis Press, 2003.

These are essential works for choosing which films you might need for inspiration and fantasies like this.

Etcetera

Anything is possible for those gifted with imagination. You can plunge yourself into a tropical atmosphere simply by hanging mosquito netting over your bed. With a little borrowing from Halloween costumes, you can create a gothic motif, turn your bedroom into a jungle or garden by arranging all the plants in your place around the bed, or go techno with TVs and video screens to create a different ambience. The important thing is obviously that these new situations should stir up your passion. What other reason is there to go to all the effort, unless at the end you are satisfied?

◉ Change the Bed

MOVE IT AROUND Among other simple changes to your environment is the location of your bed. Above all, don't hesitate to move it. Put it in another room. If you can't move the whole thing, with its heavy frame and box spring, just throw the mattress on the floor, in any corner, in the bathroom, in the hallway, or on the balcony. What's wrong with that? Nothing… although, at this point, having a futon that's easy to carry would be advantageous.

Try putting your mattress in the middle of the floor in the largest room of your place. This alone may guarantee a fun weekend. First of all, you will see things from another angle. While this may appear insignificant, it can make all the difference in the world. And it won't detract from your lovemaking.

REDECORATE After all of this consideration about moving things around, you may want to get a new bed. You might want to look for something that would serve your pleasure better.

≈ **Canopy Bed** The canopy bed is back! You can find them everywhere, especially in trendy design stores. The canopy bed has many titillating qualities. For one thing, it lets you close off the bed from the rest of the world or be selective about the view. For example, you can cloak the side facing the rest of the room and leave a large opening facing the window, creating the sense of the window as an extension of the bed. The canopy bed is also equipped with four posts. Try to remember that these posts are meant, primarily, to hold the cloth above, but they also will allow you to hang on with a firm grip while receiving thrusting. They are also good for tying your arms down while being sucked, can provide leverage for your feet when spreading your legs wide for a tonguing, and are handy for making love standing up in bed. They are truly very useful.

≈ **Round Bed** Fantasies come true! The round bed is so much a stage for having sex that one hesitates to put pillows on it and tuck in the sheets. Why would you put it anywhere but in the middle of the room? Count on it! It is impossible that the only thing you will use *this bed* for is sleeping.

≈ **Water Bed** Water beds are a little squishy, and they may be lukewarm, but they are oh-so-tempting for a scandalous siesta in a motel or for a crash landing after the high-fashion party breaks up. Water beds have not always had the best reputation, but when it comes to making love, they offer amusing possibilities: contortion, comfort, rhythm….

≈ **King-Sized Bed** King-sized beds are great for when you have friends over for late-night fun. Even when not in use as a playpen, a king-sized bed has many important advantages. It is big enough for almost anything. You can rest well instead of waking up groggy, spread out all the way, or bury yourself under the covers.

ch 2. At the House

Your apartment, your house, your building...you think you know your immediate surroundings. This is especially true of the bedroom; you think you know it because you are there every day. But in the same way that you may never truly come to know someone, even someone you have known "like family," you don't ever really know a room, a masterpiece, or a place without having found some freedom there, some liberation. So venture out and make love everywhere; it is one way to discover the world.

◉ Around Your Apartment Pounce on each other before you even get inside the apartment or take advantage of an area of your apartment complex or building that is open to public use. You will find it is very tempting.

≈ *On the Steps*
Adventures satisfying the desire to do it in a public area can easily take place in a stairwell, long extolled as a practical invention (and a great method for getting from one floor to the next, but that's not what we're talking about!). Caution! As is the case for all the situations suggested in this book, you must be ab-so-lute-ly discreet! Choose the right time, such as in the wee hours when you are stumbling home from the

nightclub, for example, and not in the afternoon when the mailman comes or the landlord is around.

The ultimate position: The stairs allow her to climb a few steps up and kneel or bend over for a tongue-'n-groove session, performed by him as he stands a step or two below. The steps may just as easily provide the compensation needed for height discrepancies, allowing for creative standing/kneeling combinations of lovemaking. And, naturally, the handrail is important as a handhold and for leaning on.

Obviously, carpeted steps are preferable, but don't pass up a marble staircase—the chill of the stone can revive the senses of the person seated upon it. But be careful! Wooden staircases can make a racket and give you splinters, so they should be avoided. The noise and shaking can wake up the whole building from the ground floor to the roof.

DIFFICULTY: Finding the right time.
PREPARATION: None; this is the definition of spontaneity.
COST: Free, unless you get caught.
PLEASURE: Quick thrill, but that's the attraction.
RISKS: Check your local penal codes.
INCONVENIENCES: Discomfort. The biggest enemy: the second hand ticking! Don't forget security, neighbors, a cold draft, splinters, etc.

≈ *In the Elevator*
This is the great classic in the quickie world. The elevator, especially at certain hours of the night, offers many possibilities. If the elevator car is traditionally narrow or small, it just means you'll have to do it on your feet.

There are two different scenarios related to elevators, and they are described below.

Daytime

A quickie in a running elevator—during the day and in a busy building—is almost stupidity, especially if the elevator stops on every floor. Only a few quick caresses are imaginable when you catch it empty, and even more stealth is required when you are not alone, due to the presence of video cameras. In the case of an elevator that can be temporarily stopped between floors, the risk may be worth considering. A false maintenance issue can yield a few minutes of precarious naughtiness. The standard is for her to press her face to one of the walls and offer her little rump to him. It is recommended that you minimize your movements lest you jostle the elevator car too much and cause a real maintenance problem or breakdown. In any case, it is best not to waste time. Adjust your attire back to normal before the doors open. This is exactly why they put mirrors in the elevator!

…and Nighttime

At night, when the building is deserted, an elevator car can become a love nest. Some modern elevators have become luxurious, with padded carpeting and reflective interiors. Even so, we advise you not to spend too long in there. You never know when a random call will come for the car, and it is better, anyway, to take advantage of the opportunity when you are already hot and bothered and the conditions are optimal. Pretend you are the night guard, and your lover has come for a quick visit during your shift. Be wary of security cameras and surveillance….

DIFFICULTY: None, except for finding the right moment.
PREPARATION: None, unless you are planning for an elevator rendezvous specifically. If that's the case, you can spend

anywhere from one hour to several weeks scoping out the perfect moment.

COST: None, unless you are arrested. Research what the amount of the fine might be.

PLEASURE: Fleeting, but, as we say often in this guide, that's part of the attraction.

RISKS: Check local penal codes.

INCONVENIENCES: Discomfort; anxiety associated with being caught; trouble walking afterward (in extreme cases).

≋ *A Special Circumstance: The Empty Apartment*

It is a common fantasy for realtors/leasing agents—when showing an existing residence—to have a brief, hot encounter with a client who comes to visit the property. One specific encounter was popularized in the film by Bernardo Bertolucci, *The Last Tango in Paris*, where an empty apartment was the setting for encounters between two potential buyers. It is worth saying that this situation is very unlikely to occur in metropolitan locations such as Paris or New York, where each apartment showing usually generates a slew of potential buyers—at least as improbable as it is that this would develop into a group thing. Let's play the roles of Marlon Brando and Marie Schneider, the actors who enjoyed each other right there on the naked floor. We hope there will be a refrigerator that is stocked with more than pats of butter.

An empty apartment offers little other than Spartan comforts, even more Spartan if the carpet has not yet been installed. In this case, it is a good idea to bring a rug or blanket to put between your skin and the floor. Making love on the floor of a large empty room is a splendid treat. He has the delight of sprawling wide open while she straddles him.

We probably don't have to tell a couple who is just moving in to a new apartment how much fun it can be to inaugurate each room. And the intimate knowledge of the apartment gathered this way will probably help you avoid small disagreements that will come along sooner or later: where the best place to put the bed is; which rooms are no good for grooming or lovemaking because the neighbors can see in (or, if you prefer, which rooms are the *best* places to shave or make love in so that everyone can see); which rooms carry sound and where your cries of passion will least disturb the neighbors.... In sum, you can learn a lot. Obviously, you can take advantage of an apartment that you visit if the realtor or leasing agent hands you the keys and waits outside while you look it over. With that time pressure, it will be more difficult to take advantage of each room, but you can try: doggie in the spare bedroom, a little grinding in the kitchen in front of the sink, some slippery business in the bathroom, and so on.

In a renovation or a building still under construction, the difficulty will be to avoid the attention of contractors or decorators. Otherwise, try it out. No need to let the dust collect in there.

DIFFICULTIES: Finding the spot.

PREPARATION: None! You're there; let's go!

COST: The realtor's commission, if you decide to buy.

PLEASURE: Hard to describe. It varies, although you can add this to the idea that you are enjoying yourself, for once, at the landlord's expense.

RISKS: None, as long as you have the only set of keys.

INCONVENIENCES: Nothing to really worry about except for dusty knees and possible splinters.

◉ All the Other Rooms of the House

Each room in a house can provide amusements, whether you share your plan with your partner or you find yourselves there together by chance or coincidence—homes of friends, step-family, etc. It would be silly not to enjoy these amusements, starting right now.

BATHROOM The clean bathroom is one of the most erotic settings in the house. Everything you need to have a bit of fun is right there, including the most important ingredient: a reason to get naked for bathing. The bathroom is, after all, the place where most people get undressed. There, it is possible to surprise your partner in the nude, finding her in a moment of quiet reflection as she brushes her hair, or catching him wearing a towel, loosely knotted at the waist, that can easily be stripped off. Sex play is just as natural in the bathroom as it is in the bedroom. The bathroom is an intimate place that has it all—nudity, comfort, body-care products, intriguing smells. Everything is just the way you like it, and this contributes to the awakening of your sensuality.

≈ *Shower*

Taking a shower together can be the beginning of a great adventure. For a couple this can be pleasant and a chance to discover each other's bodies as if for the first time. The soapy washcloth sliding over your body can be the vehicle of seduction—at once caressing, spurring desire, and encouraging you to give in to temptation. As the lather builds, so does your excitement. Trace your hands around your partner's goodies or focus on the objects of your fascination—breasts, buns, a stiff penis. (One note: some soaps can irritate sensitive areas, so don't spend too much time scrubbing.) A handheld shower wand, cleverly used, can also be useful in evoking naked lust.

The best position for having sex in the shower stall is for him to put his back against the wall and for her to turn her back to him and slowly impale herself on him. If you utterly lack imagination, remember James Bond, in the final scene of *A View to a Kill*, with Roger Moore saying to the ravishing Tanya Roberts, "That is not the soap."

DIFFICULTY: None.
PREPARATION: There you are; go for it!
COST: You'll need a plumber if the drain gets stopped up; otherwise, none.
PLEASURE: Wet. Perfect for the preliminaries or for a quickie before you really get down to business elsewhere.
RISKS: Be wary of hot water. Grab the wrong handle—not even thinking about it—and the water can burn. Be warned that the common practice of focusing a jet stream of fairly hot water on the anus or vagina can turn bad with an accidental nudge of the temperature controls! Otherwise few other risks exist.
INCONVENIENCES: Pruned skin from being in the water too long (it happens to everyone who has been in there as long as you may be). Water splashing all over the floor. Potential of ruining your partner's clothes if he is still wearing them when you pull him in. Condoms can be a challenge to apply and use in the watery environment.

Recommended Reading

The Butcher by Alina Reyes. New York: Grove Press, 1988. (Note: This title is a double entendre in French, meaning both "the butcher" and "mouthing him" or "putting him in your mouth.")

The young woman, heroine of the book *The Butcher* by Alina Reyes, is found in the shower. "I stepped over the ledge, held my hands up to the warm water, took the soap…" She washes his back and massages it. Small circles leading down to the butt cheeks.… "Then, he turned around to face me. I looked up to see his swollen manhood, his stiffening rod, right there before my eyes." The young lady continues her task, "I ran my hands over his manliness and from the base, continued toward his anus. His erection grew harder, noticeably expanding." The two lovers are obviously drenched. She continues, "…and I too was groaning, with the water of the shower beating on me, my dress tight and stuck to me like a silky second skin, the world seemed to disappear before my eyes, only his loins, and the sound of the water pounding on us and my hand stroking him.…" The butcher climaxes. "The liquid gushing out in spurts, splattering on my face and dress." Perhaps we should remember to disrobe before making love in the shower.

≈ *Bathtub*

The size of your bathtub has a lot to do with how much you will enjoy being in it together. The bigger the bathtub, the more comfortable it will be to frolic in. The tub can be used empty or full. When empty, it allows for numerous amusements: doggie over the handles, hands on the rails, her straddling him lying on the bottom.… In a full tub, things change very quickly depending on the waves you make! Even so, the same positions apply. Don't forget that, since the dawn of time, bathing has been part of erotic traditions where each partner has his and her role to play. It is here that lovers groom and prepare each other for lovemaking; here they dote on each other, cleanse each other, and put their scent on each other. One should always have a bottle of scented bubble bath on hand, a back scrubber, soft washcloths, and an exfoliant.... That's it.

DIFFICULTY: None

PREPARATION: Worst case: the time it takes to run a bath.

COST: Nothing, unless you flood the place.

PLEASURE: Perfect.

RISKS: Burns—see "Shower." Also, some bath products can irritate sensitive skin, so choose bubble bath or bath scents carefully.

INCONVENIENCES: Splashing water, humidity overdose.

special circumstance: public showers

"It was in the showers at the city college one Sunday morning, and there was no one in sight. We were totally alone in the corridor between his dormitory and the showers, where everyone runs around with nothing on. We had spent a lot of time in bed already this weekend; I'd almost forgotten about the showers, their soap dispensers aligned with the industrial mirrors. When there was water, it wasn't always hot; we started by washing together, then I remember sucking him for the first time, the soapy water running out of my hair down my face and over my thighs. A few minutes later, still naked, I found myself flat on my stomach in this crude shower. He was on top of me, going in and out of my proffered ass. Face in the ground, arms spread, breasts and belly pressed to the cold, wet tile. I wouldn't trade it for the nicest bed of all time." — Sarah

≈ *Laundry Room*

The laundry room is equipped with a very tempting appliance, the washing machine. It has a quality that you'd be crazy not to take advantage of: It vibrates! She can sit on the machine while it is running, bringing her hips at the edge to receive him, standing facing her. The combined effects of him going in and out with the jostling of the machine, especially at a climactic plateau, can set her bottom on fire. If that doesn't work, you can always try making love in a laundry basket.

DIFFICULTY: Locating or having a laundry room.
PREPARATION: None. There you are; go for it!
COST: Nothing.
PLEASURE: Amusing; use the "large load" cycle, no doubt.
RISKS: None.
INCONVENIENCES: Getting dirty when you come to do the wash.

≈ *Restrooms*

They are everywhere—in most public places, restaurants, offices, airports, and train stations. The doors usually lock, and there's always a free seat. It is nearly ideal, and it is practical.... The best position: He is seated on the throne; she is straddling him, facing toward him or away. One can easily see her standing, one foot up on the toilet, offering her rump to him as he stands behind her with a firm grip on her hips. Although you don't always have to look for a clean restroom, you may be more comfortable at home. Consider that it can be fun to take advantage of the bathroom in any house, even when visiting the in-laws for example.

Be careful of public toilets that are frequently used. However, some like it even better when the door is open to surprises.

DIFFICULTY: The hardest part is getting both of you into the restroom without someone noticing. Usually restrooms are not unisex.
PREPARATION: Once you're in, go for it!
COST: None unless caught; check local penal codes.
PLEASURE: The unique quality of the experience.
RISKS: Necessarily secretive or you risk being accused of public indecency.
INCONVENIENCES: Germs—but you can wash your hands when you leave. Be wary of the well-used public restroom.

≈ *Kitchen*

Everyone knows food and sex are closely tied together. With this adventure, we're going to have sex at the table, during the meal. So clear the table.

Now the glassware, plates, and silverware are scattered on the floor; she is laid on the table like the next course and will be consumed right there, just like in the scene from *The Postman Always Rings Twice*. He will devour her like a second dessert, perhaps even covering her in whipped cream, powdered sugar, chocolate sauce, and nuts—or some combination of these—as he pleases. It is more likely that he will choose to slurp champagne from the crease formed where the thighs and mound meet. Oh, yes, you can. You go right ahead and play hide the salami. Great admirers of Middle-Eastern romance have learned that for this experience, "the man is seated table high, penis taut and ready, the woman positions herself above him, her lips wrapped around him and her lips on his lips; they taste of each other and taste pleasure to the core...."

DIFFICULTY: At home, there are no difficulties. Otherwise, there's no telling.

PREPARATION: Apparently, it is a spontaneous gesture, unless you can't wait to set the table.

COST: Broken glasses and plates.

PLEASURE: Welcome to the best buffet on earth! Truly. And no etiquette is required.

RISKS: Indigestion.

INCONVENIENCES: Shopping for more glasses and dinnerware; food splattered in the dining room.

at the table with Catherine Millet, author of The Sexual Life of Catherine M.

Catherine Millet recalls with great detail the adventures she had in several swingers' clubs somewhere in a rustic neighborhood of Paris. Discussing the furniture being used, she warns of a particular concern of hers involving a rustic table: "There were times I was thrown down on the table in such a way that I had to grab onto its sides with both hands, and for a long time I had a semi-permanent abrasion on my back, right above my coccyx, where my vertebral column rubbed against the rough wood." Fair warning!

— Catherine Millet, *The Sexual Life of Catherine M.*

≈ *Balconies and Terraces*

One of two situations: In the first, the balcony is open to street view and is easily seen by the neighbors; in the second, the balcony is high enough up that the view is blocked, and there is some privacy screen blocking out the neighbors. In the first scenario, fooling around will be limited and best done only during the wee hours of the night. In the second instance, the only question is, "Why didn't we think of this before?"

Making love on the balcony is refreshing. The balcony is open air, outdoors, and two steps from the drawing room. For more elaborate games, we recommend dressing it up for comfort. Cushions and blankets can make a soft pad, shield you from view, or prop you up if that's your thing—it is for you to decide what fantasy to make your own, like the first scene of Hitchcock's *Rear Window*, in which a pajama-wearing couple wakes each other up on their terrace.

Your open-air love nest may be used just like a bed, offering the same comforts, but with one or two advantages. The hard floor makes any mattress more firm and stable. Thrusts carry more force; penetration is fresher and deeper. She, lying on her back, will be happy to affirm this. He may also notice the plusses of having his prize pinned down to something firm. When straddling him, she will also notice the various pleasurable effects caused by bouncing on a hard saddle. What's more, there is the great open sky above you, the noises of the street and the city, the sunshine pouring over your skin or the moon and stars lighting the night. The little plants you may keep out there show a different side of themselves when seen from lying down, as if they are bigger and thicker. Note that because of the firm surface, doing it doggy style may be a little rough on the knees.

A private balcony, or one bathed in complete darkness, offers still more possibilities. She can put her hands up against the wall, facing it with her legs spread, and lean into his invigorated thrusts while the breeze blows between their legs.

Fellatio and cunnilingus will also ascend to a new level in the open air. He can put his back to the wall and peer out into the distance or down at the display of her blowing his…mind, on top of the world. He can do just the same for her, with her back against the wall, one foot on his shoulder while he tongues her sex.

DIFFICULTIES: Accessing a private balcony.

PREPARATION: A little sweeping and setting up, but nothing more.

COST: The price of some geraniums and maybe a rug or a curtain.

PLEASURE: Perfect, maximum enjoyment; all the advantages of making love in the great outdoors without the hassle of having to sit in traffic to get there.

RISK: Being seen; being heard. You have to be discreet. Be aware of public indecency laws.

INCONVENIENCES: Nothing serious.

the balcony

> "We threw two rugs we bought while traveling on the floor of our balcony. It must have been noon on a Sunday; the weather was beautiful, and we both laid down on them in our clothes to see if the floor was soft enough. The wall that rises to the handrail gave us privacy from the apartment buildings across from us. Still, we

kept some skimpy clothes on just in case the neighbors in the upper floors could see over the edge. So there we were, lying on the ground. Tina stretched out, lying down with her back to me; she was wearing a long skirt with thick fabric and stockings…so I pulled her skirt up and slipped beneath to fondle and penetrate her. We made love quietly. I tried to reach as far as I could inside her. Each muted thrust drew a muffled groan from deep within her. On that day, we took it back inside, more or less clutching our loose clothing as we stumbled back into the bed.

"Since then, we often find ourselves visiting the balcony at night, and we are both happy, in retrospect, that we bought those rugs." — Peter

SOLDIERS FOR THE SAKE OF THE BOUDOIR The boudoir, which has pretty much disappeared from homes, had the unique charm of being made "just for that"! In 1758 a work titled *La petite maison* (*The Little House*) by Jean-François de Bastide described some of the eccentricities and adventures of the soap-operatic aristocracy. The boudoir, a room more private and intimate than the sitting room, yet separate and distinct from the bedroom, was glorified as the setting for everything unrefined. "All the walls were covered with mirrors, the seams between them masked with faux tree trunks.…" In the middle of the room was a large ottoman, "a kind of a bed," which served its purpose. One received lovers here, and the most sought after were thrown down "on the voluptuous cushion, rich with gallantry.…"

THE TWENTY-FIRST-CENTURY BOUDOIR When you are looking at a new apartment—no matter what its size—or a home, either in town or in the country, you should immediately consider the possible locations for your "boudoir." It can be a dedicated space or a spot that you can screen off in a few short minutes.

≈ *In the Home*

A boudoir in an apartment should consist of at least a daybed, nice couch, or futon—with large mirrors positioned around it to capture the spectacle that takes place there—with a curtain, screen, or plants to define the space. You can set it up almost anywhere, perhaps in your studio, a nook, a bay window, an alcove; any corner with enough room for a small bed should be investigated. A futon mattress, kept elsewhere when not in use, can work just as well. The mirrors should stand tall from the ground, preferably, and the lighting should be adjustable as well.

Everything else in terms of décor is whatever you want it to be. You could, for instance, go with an Asian motif, with a rug and pillows, or pretend it is a cabin in the woods with rustic accents, or choose a more urban, trashy flavor, or even a torture chamber. Research the décor used in old brothels for inspiration. The important thing is that this space inspires you, that it is comfortable, and that no one, except for those you invite to your boudoir, can tell why you brought them there.

≈ *Outside*

You can set up your boudoir outside just as well, on the balcony, terrace, or in the garden gazebo. The choice will have a lot to do with the amount of privacy you require. You can use the tool shed, the gazebo, a tent, or the pool house, or you can form your boudoir from more organic elements, like hay bales or a corner of the yard where the fences meet. The important thing is still that your boudoir is comfortable and easy to set up or close off for privacy. Mirrors, too, will be very welcome, so find some that are easy to carry or invent some reason to have them there. The more sophisticated thinkers might even plant bushes, imagining that it will eventually grow and be integrated into this boudoir one day. Are you really going to wait for the young vines on the gazebo to bloom?

You can even have a separate shelter for your secret desires. A workshop of sorts, a large shed or small barn that only needs a little sprucing up to make it more inviting. What's more, you can even choose which fox gets a key to your hen house.

THE BOUDOIR RECIPE
- mirrors
- scented candles
- condoms; lubrication; sexy underwear kept in an elegant box with a lid
- your favorite sex toys
- a cooler or mini-bar for when you are thirsty before…and after
- something you can wear that hides your nudity but allows you to have sex without taking it completely off: a robe, dressing gown, etc.
- eventually, a DVD player stocked with your favorite sexy movies, but no phones—cellular or otherwise!

◎ The Furniture Any furniture, from the armoire to the buffet to an end table can offer service as something you can lean against or sit on as you explore new possibilities with the various positions you thought you had worn out completely. Furnishings, with their great variety of forms, are our friends. We suggest the purchase of a few in particular.

THE GREAT CLASSICS The following pieces of furniture can really be fun to use.

≈ *Chair*

There are many advantages to making love in a chair. First of all, you can find one just about anywhere. Most likely, it has been ready to serve and quite assuredly used for everyday applications, as well as your erotic exploits during its full life of surprises and joys. Unfortunately, the possibilities it offers are not very numerous. He may sit upon it with his back pressed to the backrest and allow her to prove her skills. In two or three movements, she can have his pants undone and his penis hardening in her hand as she saddles up for a rodeo ride with her legs thrown wide and his face buried in her breasts. Then, pitching herself up onto the balls of her feet, she can swirl her basin in pretty ways until they both juice all over each other. He can participate nicely by fondling her breasts and lifting or squeezing her bottom at just the right moments.

In the priceless anonymous work *Art de foutre en quarante manières* (Forty Ways to F*ck), the author describes a position called, "The Mystery Girl," in which "The f*cker sits in a chair and the lady climbs up to sit in his lap but with her back to him; then she reaches under her skirt, seizes his happy stick to line it up with her hole of choice, and buries it into place with the force of her own weight…." The author goes on to mention that this position can be useful to know for pleasant distractions: "In the carriage, returning from an evening out, a show, or the ball; how many women have been f*cked this way, some right in front of mommy dearest."

So much for the basics. The chair can also be used in other ways. It can facilitate penetration in standing positions. Madame puts one foot up on the seat and so doing rocks her hips to one side giving easier access to her moist and tempting sex.

≈ *Bench*

A simple bench with no backrest, having a solid stance and smooth surface that leaves no real risk of getting splinters, is one of the more indispensable objects every couple should have.

Lying on his back, sex firm and high, he becomes the perfect perch for Madame to straddle; standing above him she can feel her legs burn with the vigorous workout she is getting. She can put her hands on his chest and lean over him or remain upright for even fuller penetration. He has only to be there and manage not to fall off the bench.

Variation: She can stand over him facing the other way while he points himself in the right direction. She can lie on her stomach on the bench offering her rump up to him, and he can mount her from a position where he is standing over her with his legs on either side. This position can also be very convenient for anal sex.

The bench can serve just as well for other types of "country cooking," like those suggested in Dr. A. S. Lagail's *Les paradis charnels* (Carnal Delights). "The lady is lying on the bench, the man standing above her with his legs wide, nearly seated on her bosom, he throttles his member back and forth between her breasts as she squeezes them together, expertly creating a slippery embrace for their mutual delight."

SPECIFIC RISKS: Almost none, if you don't have to worry about splinters. At least as long as you don't try to use a school bench "in a school" and therefore....

≈ Table

Love play under the table is only imaginable if the table is covered with a tablecloth that falls all the way to the floor. In this case, the space under the table can become a naughty love nest at a cocktail party or social function that grows boring. Try not to think about it too much.

The great classic sexual fantasy, "love under the table," is getting oral sex from a her or him who is hidden beneath the tablecloth on their knees while he or she is seated at the table trying to play it cool like nothing is happening.

Making love on the table is also a classic, with the table at just the right height for her to perch her hips on the edge, offering him a choice of entries.

SPECIFIC RISKS: The table could collapse under your weight.

≈ Stools

Bar stools and footstools are our friends. You should always have one available so that he can sit on it and she can straddle him there. Sometimes it is even better to have a pair, so that she can prop each of her feet up with her legs spread wide, allowing him to easily slide between them. A bar stool can serve well as something she might lean on or bend over, standing with her legs spread and knees locked so that her lovely bottom is projecting from the perpendicular angle formed by her legs and torso at the waist. Without a doubt, stools are our friends.

≈ *Wingback Chairs and Loveseats*

Now this is exactly what you should have at your place—a wingback chair, a love seat, divan, sofa.... These furnishings are made for sex! They beckon you from behind the closed door of your bedroom, to the sitting room, the waiting room, the lobby, or anywhere there isn't a bed. All the positions you really like are warmer in a wingback; all the love you crave is waiting in a loveseat. Just take a look at all the artwork from the eighteenth century: the dainty young bride of the marquis, lounging seductively across a divan, scenes of love play on the lush cushioned sofas.... What more can be said, except that these furnishings should be chosen with their "true" function in mind. Comfortable, cushy, washable.... All kinds of these wonderful pieces of furniture are available, from convertible couches to multisectionals with reclining backs.

General Concerns for Using Furniture

DIFFICULTY: Insignificant.
PREPARATION: None.
COST: The sale price of the furniture, obviously.
PLEASURE: Assuredly different every time.
RISKS: Falling off is a risk, but it is not that far to the floor.
INCONVENIENCES: Cramps and twisting, but we don't need to go into detail on how that happens.

≈ *The Closet and the Pantry!*

People don't take enough advantage of a walk-in closet. Why not enjoy a toss among the dry cleaning and the hangers? Go ahead—it is fun. There's not a lot of room, but it is all in step with the bourgeois farce of hiding your lover in the closet so as not to get caught in an adulterous affair. Instead of hiding there, why not jump in together!

SOME TYPES OF FURNISHINGS THAT YOU CAN FORGET ABOUT USING, OR PLAN ON THROWING AWAY

- Rolling bar or dessert cart: These are too fragile.
- Formal seating and chairs with worn or delicate fabrics such as silk: These are easily split or torn.
- Expensive art-deco furniture: unique: Do not damage even in the name of good times.
- Kitchen buffets: Watch out for forks and knives in the drawers.
- Ovens and stoves: Are you sure that the burners are cool?
- Handmade furniture—no matter what kind!—that you made yourself: It would be a shame to ruin something you worked so hard to assemble.

SOME UNIQUE PIECES When you come back from the consignment store with a strange piece of furniture, we'll explain how to take advantage of it.

≈ *Church Pew*

Church pews are designed as a low seat bench with a pad in front that you can kneel on and a rail you can lean on in prayer. In this voluptuous position of reverence, forearms braced on the rail, lewd images do not occur to you. Oh, well, excuse me, quickly flip to another chapter! This lovely object can usually be found in a used surplus furniture warehouse. If your friends get curious as to why you have such a thing, tell them it is the first in a collection of religious objects. Others—which are more practical—will present themselves. Church pews facilitate anal penetration. There! Someone had to say it. It encourages her to take tempting positions that offer up her bottom. The pew also inspires fantasies about full confession. One of the lovers plays the role of the confessor, making up steamy sexual "transgressions" or using stories torn from an erotic book of sex fantasies. The rest depends on your version of "penitence."

Recommended Reading
Les mystères du confessional (The Secrets of the Confessional) by Bouvier (Monseigneur). Levallois Perret, France: Filipacchi, 1974.

≈ *Daybed or Exam Chair*
Andrea de Nerciat, a famous French romance writer from the eighteenth century, describes a strange furnishing "that is neither a sofa, nor a love seat, but a low-slung bed, six feet long, having only a quilted cushion between the fabric and the frame, a raised end to support the head of a person and a sloping end where the cushion tapers off to a foot rest...." In Europe we call this a contemporary daybed or sometimes a *recamier*. It is ideal for displaying the contours of the naked form and for enjoying that form with your eyes, mouth, and hands, whether day or night.

An exam chair is a furnishing designed to support a woman who is lying on it from the nape of her neck to the small of her back; the legs are supported by stirrups or foot pedals that bend the knees and part the legs, determining the angle of the thighs. It is easy to see what advantages this position has for playing between her legs. Why not play doctor? Why not use equipment specifically designed for such fun and games? Why not shop for and decorate your place with something you can *really* use? He could play her extremely friendly gynecologist or the kindly family physician charged with helping her achieve deeper orgasms. She could be his very imaginative proctologist or the urologist charged with enlarging his erection.

Ch 3. At Work

> "I have methodically marked all the hot spots for sex in the workplace."
> — Catherine Millet, *The Sexual Life of Catherine M.*

◎ At the Office An article published by the Associated French Press on June 14, 2002, reveals that 61 percent of women say, "Flirting in the work place is good for morale," and that 83 percent of them feel flattered when someone makes a pass at them. More interestingly, 10 percent of the females surveyed remember having a fling with their boss, and 11 percent of these ultimately married him. All notions of rank aside, three out of four women report flirting with their coworkers, and 28 percent of these follow through on their advances with sexual relations…at work. American women responding to a *Playboy* questionnaire report that two thirds have fantasized about having sex in the workplace. The women agree that their choice is to be right on top of the desk, while the men prefer the idea of using the chair instead.

≈ *Your Own Office*

When you are the boss, who cares! You have all the advantages you need for a dazzling sex life. The boss-man or the boss-lady can bring in whomever they want, usually through the side door. He or she can take all the time they want to seal the deal and even more if they want to make sure the coast is clear. That is to say, the only real work to be done here after hours is in deciding which piece of furniture looks the most tempting. The waiting-room bench, a club chair in the meeting room, the swiveling and rocking secretary's seat, the conference table, the reception desk countertop, or your own desk—it's all fair game.

The Biggest Risk: Getting accused of sexual harassment: This is a fine line to walk with the law. You must be absolutely sure that the desire is mutual. Other than that, just don't let anyone see you doing it. The dynamics are very different from those surrounding dating, and they become more and more pronounced the further you descend through the employee ranks. Having sex at work is an aggressively risky activity. Every person you work with can potentially find out the goods on you....

Alternatively, have your lover come to your office and act out the work fantasy of your choice. Here, the only risk is getting caught by an unsuspecting coworker who is working late or retrieving her forgotten briefcase after hours.

≋ *Office Chair*
The office chair, with its rolling casters, its height adjustment lever, and its swivel-back support, has long been a favorite of the libertine. The possibilities offered by this piece of furniture are many. It combines the usability of a stiff-backed chair with the flexibility of motion afforded by something like a hammock or a barber's chair. He can position himself firmly behind her while she kneels in the seat leaning over the backrest, and once he has good contact, he can use his grip to roll her back

and forth, making his thrusts more thunderous, or he can rock her up and down or side to side for different angles of penetration. All are good fun. Just hope no one bursts through the door without an appointment, and remember to savor the thrill!

closing time for the day shift

"We had been sleeping together for a few nights, once or twice a week, and working together in the same large office. No one doubted we were more than friends and colleagues. One night, we were the last ones to leave the office, there was no one left on the whole floor, everything was dimly lit in the shadowy building. We got all the way to the elevator before we both noticed it at the same time; with a look, we both made a U-turn and raced back to an empty room to take advantage of the darkness. We pressed each other against the door in a passionate embrace. I slipped my hand under her skirt to get two fingers inside of her; she had already freed me from my pants and was jerking me hard. She got down on her knees, taking my sex in her mouth…and that was just when we heard the elevator begin its trip up from the ground floor. She wasn't going to stop for the elevator or anything else—which was too bad because I came in her mouth almost right away…. Two minutes later, we were saying goodnight to the night watchman. Only after we were on the bus did we think to look at each other for visible evidence of 'our little scandal.'" — Michael

≈ In Front of the Office Window

Modern high-rise office buildings tend to have two distinct advantages; they rise high above other buildings around them and their façade is clad in floor-to-ceiling tinted windows. So making love on the top floors, facing out the window, gives one an unimaginable thrill…that of ejaculation and orgasm from the dominant vantage of having the world at your feet. No one else can see you from the outside. My friends, let me beg you to double-check! Are you sure you locked the door?

> "My date, whom I met at his office overlooking the rue de Rennes, agreed when I told him I wanted to give him head in front of the windows that make the exterior of the building; and the euphoric excitement that rose up in me as I was on my knees blowing him in the filtered light really was special for us both."
> — Catherine Millet, *The Sexual Life of Catherine M.*

≈ The Filing Room

The mythical room that, unfortunately, not all offices still possess.

Your best chance: designated holidays. Wait until the evening when the last stragglers have punched out and the night security has not yet arrived. Even in these modern times, it is wise to pay attention to the lessons of old.

> "When you are afraid of getting caught with your pants down, the door just barely cracked so your girl can keep an eye on the elevator and you can listen for anyone approaching, her mind in the gutter with you between her legs, there is

an urgency to the whole thing that gives you a surge of strength. It would truly be a travesty to get busted, right at the pinnacle of pleasure, and after all the precautions you took."

— From the anonymous work *Art de foutre en quarante manières* (Forty Ways to F*ck)

≈ *Lesson Learned: The Photocopier*

Here's one piece of equipment you should avoid at all costs. It is already rickety from being moved from upstairs, it jams all the time, and you know it will break if you use it to prop up that booty to just the right height. What's more, you've heard jokes about couples getting caught when they mash the copy button accidentally but forget to take the copies with them when they finish. Want everyone at work to know what tattoos you have? Frightening!

DIFFICULTY: Having sex at the office, though possible, remains largely the stuff of fantasies, except when the office is closed for holidays. If that's your idea of a holiday then bring dessert toppings—why not really go wild?

PREPARATION: Weeks of planning for just the right place and just the right time. Or exactly the opposite, a spontaneous quickie, where you pounce on each other before you even think about it; all you need is just one dirty glance at the coffee station.

COST: Your job if you get caught.

PLEASURE: Perfect. In general, having sex at work is the realization of a long-held fantasy, finally tapping the ass of the secretary or that hot coworker that you've flirted with for a long time.

RISK: Check local sexual harassment codes. Other risks include reprimand, your promotion, being ridiculed, and having your reputation destroyed.

INCONVENIENCES: Ditto.

Business

≈ Small Business and Boutique

The back of a boutique offers lots of opportunities. It is enough to be friendly with the owner or some of the employees. Each little shop has its specialty and sometimes in a torrid encounter you get something extra—like covered in grease if you have a taste for the butcher's meat or, if your mechanic revs your engine, a different kind of grease.

≈ Department Stores

If you are getting the ride of your life in one of the dressing rooms at Macy's, don't shout that you're coming. That would cause a terrible scandal. Even today, a quickie in the dressing room remains one of the major fantasies for the exhibitionists among us. It used to be that it wasn't really that hard to get away with, but modern security and procedures aimed at preventing shoplifting make it close to impossible to go unnoticed. Unfortunately, there is usually a camera in the hallway in front of the changing rooms. The salespeople watch who goes in and comes out.... The ideal situation is to pick up one of the girls who works there and is supposed to keep people from being naughty.

DIFFICULTY: There is no way of knowing, since it is basically impossible to predict what the complications in this type of situation might be.

PREPARATION: If, despite everything noted here, there is an opportunity, strike while the iron is hot and be quick!!
COST: Bail if you get caught.
PLEASURE: The quickest of quickies.
RISK: Parole for first-time offenders, if you are lucky, and a fine.
INCONVENIENCES: Trying to explain to the retailer how you mussed up those pants so badly just by trying them on.

◎ A Few Special Professions

≈ *Dentist's Chair*

Dentists are just about the only people who can make full use of an object the rest of us fantasize about—at least so long as "the rest of us" don't have toothaches: the dentist's chair. This very specialized chair is adjustable in so many ways that the person in it can lie comfortably in all kinds of positions. In general, the chair supports positions where the feet are elevated and the mouth is very accessible, which already gives us many titillating ideas. What's more, the chair is undeniably comfortable, much more so than a gynecological chair. She can extend her legs fully and more easily hold her own legs spread wide open for him. With the chair's remote in hand, he can effortlessly adjust the device to any position that suits him. That is, until she puts him in the chair and takes matters into her own hands. The only problem is that you have to sleep with, or be, a dentist.

≈ *OB/GYN Chairs*

And since we're talking about it, gynecologists also use an object that gives ideas to even the most innocent young women who visit for appointments. This doctor's chair is irksome, but it allows one to lie on her back and spread her legs wide, thus enabling "the doctor" to see small details of the body's form more closely and make a thorough examination with the mouth or hands. However, the same problem exists as above: You have to convince a gynecologist to let you borrow his or her chair.

≋ *Nurse! Oh, Nurse!*

If you listen to the talk in the locker room, you won't need further instructions. All the same, anyone can put on a nursing uniform. How about a revealing top that gives a great view of a bulging chest? To dream! Medical personnel have access to all sorts of tools, furnishings, and stuff you can play with: speculums, thermometers, gurneys, adjustable hospital beds....

ch 4. In Town

> "Who hasn't dreamt of wild sex, with your feet up in the air, at everyday places you innocently visit?"
> — Catherine Millet, *The Sexual Life of Catherine M.*

Christening an innocent place—oh, to dream of it—but only if you don't get caught! As we begin a discussion on taking risks, remember that public places are not really intended for this kind of activity. So be careful!

◉ Out in the Open! Pornographic scenes filmed in well-known locations are classic and are even a subcategory of X-rated cinema. As such, filmmakers offer us scenes of fellatio and acrobatic penetrations in the crowded Venetian carnival or on the steps of the Eiffel Tower. Caution, dear adventurous friends! These scenes were possible only with an army of assistants shielding the actors from view and keeping the public back. It is a job.

≈ *In the Street*

Making love in the street is imaginable only in the darkest hours of the night, on the quietest streets, in the sleepiest towns.... Even then, there is always a chance of encountering a sleepless neighbor, a group of kids roaming around, or a patrolman on the night shift. She must wear something simple with easy access and panties that can be pulled aside; pants never work. He takes her in a standing position, facing her, shielding her body by pressing her back to a wall. He would do well to wear a large jacket or raincoat, so that, from a distance, it might appear as nothing more than a long kiss goodnight.

DIFFICULTY: Not being seen, not getting caught, performing well despite the anxiety. Unless anxiety makes you hot and horny.

PREPARATION: Pick the right spot and then "get it while the getting is good," according to the suggestions made.

COST: Nothing, unless you are caught.

PLEASURE: Dangerous and forbidden—it has to be quick and nasty.

RISKS: Check local penal codes.

INCONVENIENCES: Having a bucket of water (or worse) dumped on you. (At least that was a fear in old European villages with open sewers.)

≈ *Covered Doorways*

Here's a great classic of furtive love. Since the dawn of cities, making love in a covered doorway has been a commonly enjoyed quickie among young, lusty urbanites. Things have, unfortunately, gotten a little more complicated since the invention of keypad entries and video/intercom. Today, your best bet is a shadowy and obscured doorway that is recessed into the façade of a building on a street that gets no traffic late at night. It is important that you are in a place that is practically deserted and that there is no motion detector or security light that will suddenly click on. She slips into the shadowy darkness and presses her back to the wall, lifting one leg to give him the best ease of penetration and movement. We cannot stress enough how important it is to be wearing garments that can be adjusted quickly to cover you or hide his swollen bulge.

DIFFICULTIES: Few, as at night it is relatively easy.
PREPARATION: When the moment arrives, go for it.
COST: Nothing, unless you get caught.
RISKS: Check local penal codes.
INCONVENIENCES: Doormen, neighbors, insomniacs, garbage cans, and stray cats.

parking garage

"It was a complicated time for us. She lived in a room in a dormitory that did not allow male visitors. Sometimes she came over to my place and on these nights, I would walk her home late at night to the dorm. Though we spent much of the two preceding days having sex together, we both wanted more. I started to press her against the wall in a covered doorway, but she took me by the hand and I thought she was scared of getting caught in this little empty side street. Actually, she was leading me to a kind of parking deck, or maybe it was a building still under construction, only a few steps away. The guard booth was abandoned, and we walked down the parking ramp into the shadows between decks. It was black, and faintly disagreeable odors drifted from below. She pulled up her skirt and put her hands against the wall, offering me her pretty little ass, which I began to penetrate with a frenzy. We both came in

the space of a few seconds with only three or four violent thrusts, which made a slapping noise that echoed through our bodies...." — Mario

≈ *In Public Parks*

It depends on the size of the park. Some green spaces are forestlike, containing groves, brush, and tall hedges. It can be as difficult to navigate as a thicket, but at least there isn't a park ranger behind every tree.

See for yourself.

≈ *Phone Booth*

Private phone booths are disappearing. Too bad! At night, this little shelter provides innocent fun. Making out standing there, she can pretend to make a call while he taps the line....

◉ Wedged Between a Few Walls...but Well out of Sight!

≈ *In a Sex Shop*

The shopkeepers in these types of establishments know that you can only get away with it if they allow you to. Hence, it is almost impossible for two people to get into one view cabin or peep-show booth. However, many larger establishments offer "couples booths," which provide obvious uses. Containing a bench seat where couples can generally sit together, these booths can be compact, leading to all sorts of acrobatic positions. Viewing booths are usually equipped with a video screen that lets you zap between dozens of pornographic films. It will be hard to concentrate on the video though! It is better to choose a booth that lets you see the whole movie (although you can leave when you like after your short stay). You should think about which film will work best. Obviously, you'll want to consider what images you desire to view while canoodling and how a low-budget production might be just the thing for the occasion. Watch out, though. Some of these businesses hope that their clients will be exhibitionists, or even promiscuous, in a way that caters to the men who are there alone.

peep shows, as seen by catherine millet

"Go to the back of the shop where the peep show is [located]; it is like the dressing room in a theater. One finds himself plunged into obscurity in the circular hall that gives access to the booths. There are no tips for the strippers; instead one has to insert coins into a slot to get the window to stay open; [there is] a window behind which there is a girl or a couple who slither in erotic contortions so slowly it is surreal. It is so dark in the booth that I have never been able to see what is there, even the walls; it is like sitting in a void. From the stage, there is always a dim light, muted, that outlines the base of the member I have taken in my mouth, and it seems that the only thing I can see is the hump of flesh sprinkled with prickly hairs that I am swallowing down my throat. [...] Just after entering the booth, we grope each other blindly, eyes directed toward the spectacle that we pay to see. And we both agree that the stripper has a pretty pussy."

— Catherine Millet, *The Sexual Life of Catherine M.*

DIFFICULTY: Daring to go in for sex. Otherwise, it is a snap.
PREPARATION: Getting your courage up.
COST: The coinage for the viewing booth.
PLEASURE: Fleeting, uncomfortable, trashy.
RISKS: Being frightened by how filthy the booth is in some places. Voyeurs.
INCONVENIENCES: Stepping out of the booth to see there is a line of people waiting—pissed off—and having to wade through them to get out.

Recommended Viewing

7 ans de mariage (Seven Years of Marriage) by Didier Bourdon and Dominique Coubes, for the scene set in the basement of a Parisian sex shop. CiBy 2000, 2003.

≈ *At the Public Pool*

The changing rooms at the pool are also a favorite place for amateurs in the art of the quickie. It goes without saying that the pool staff will not openly tolerate sex in the changing rooms, but it can be done covertly. A swim instructor, interviewed by a men's fitness magazine, admitted that the sex is always in "uncomfortable positions"; it seems his happy encounters usually occur in a small dressing room. The only advantage in this situation is the relative quasi-nudity of swimwear. Getting to it won't require a lot of stripping. Really, you don't even have to take your suit off. The first problem: slipping into a dressing room together without attracting attention. The second problem: remaining undetected while getting it on. Often, the dressing rooms have doors that don't extend all the way to the floor, so it is therefore very important to do your research and visit as many pools as it takes to find a facility that offers enough cover for you to try to get away with it. If there is a small bench there, it might help you achieve different positions as she finds ways to lean or sit on it, bent over or stepping up on it. If not, there is only one option, standing, with her pressed against the wall, hoping that it will hold against his efforts.

DIFFICULTY: Finding the right dressing room.

PREPARATION: Waiting for the dressing room to become vacant.

COST: The fee for entry to the facility and dressing rooms.

PLEASURE: Brief, but intense, depending on the size of the dressing room.

RISKS: Knocking over the dressing room wall.

INCONVENIENCES: Exiting the dressing room to find other patrons waiting—pissed off—and the lifeguard ready to throw you out.

≈ *Fitness Club*

This is without a doubt one of the best places for having fun, even though it is so rarely deserted. Everything you could want is there! Locker rooms, often much more spacious than those at the pool, allow for a more leisurely tryst after your workout. The showers or the sauna also can be a great place for your rendezvous, and the features of these offer advantages for your exploits. Simply put, the fitness gym is just about the closest thing you can find to a swingers club. Once again, the trick is to avoid prying eyes. Once you find you are alone, then you can really work up a sweat.

Most of the muscle-ripping equipment found at the gym can be used to your advantage. The parallel bars allow her to suspend herself with her legs spread wide while he slides between them; wall bars allow you to attach yourself or someone else to the wall in all sorts of fun positions, arching the back, raising the pelvis, and angling the hips in unusual ways; the vaulting horse invites you to ride together; the floor exercise area can be as soft as a bed; and many of the Nautilus machines have benches where he can recline while she straddles him. All you could want is there, ready for use, your trainer urging you on, and those who have the keys, who can let you in after-hours, have just the thing to make you feel tight and fit.

DIFFICULTIES: Seducing someone who has the keys.
PREPARATIONS: Seducing someone who has the keys.
COST: Membership and the time it takes to seduce someone who has the keys.
PLEASURE: The pleasures one might know with a gymnast.
RISKS: Getting kicked out of the gym for breaking the rules or screwing around.
INCONVENIENCES: All the meatheads who are the friends with someone who has the keys.

Recommended Viewing

To get a convincing look at all the possibilities offered by the equipment at the gym, study X-rated films on "working out," like John Stagliano's *Buttman's Ultimate Workout*. Evil Angel, 1990.

≋ *In Church*

> "To enter this chapel, you must be on your knees,
> And you must hold a candlestick with no wick if
> you please." — Country rhyme

In one of the big scandals of 2003, a local radio station purported to have recorded and broadcast the moans of a couple having sex while tucked away in Saint Patrick's Cathedral, New York—unbelievably, while Mass was being held. In real life, however tempting it may be, no one would dare such a thing. More believably, find a small church that has been abandoned or that no one goes to anymore. There will be less risk of divine retribution like in the old, gory horror films of the 1970s. The best place has to be the confessional. It is closed off, you can get down on your knees—do your penitence, for real—and close the curtain behind you....

DIFFICULTY: Finding yourselves in a tiny country church that is isolated and abandoned, or in an immense—and empty—urban cathedral is hard to imagine.

PREPARATION: Nothing, besides overcoming your sense of guilt. Get it while the getting is good!

COST: Eternity in Hell to start with.

PLEASURE: Forbidden.

RISKS: Not just Hell, but the wrath of the law.

INCONVENIENCES: Catching a cold—it is usually drafty—and a guilty conscience.

≈ *In the Catacombs*

Catacombs have always attracted amateur fetishists who are slightly more extreme.

≈ *Museums and Historic Monuments*

No matter how much Catherine Millet or Pierre Louÿs pretend to extol lovemaking in museums, today it is practically impossible. Still, never say never. In the Louvre, in front of the *Mona Lisa*, is obviously not a good choice, but what about behind a pillar away from the usher's post in a room of medieval housewares that is rarely visited? Unfortunately, it is always the rooms that would be the most comfortable—like the queen's bedroom with that tempting little bed, the boudoir of the countess with its sofa that begs to be tried out at least once—that are frequented by the most guards. The very few places it would be possible are inconvenient: the machine room where the escalators are operated, a corner of the rampart where brambles are growing....

DIFFICULTIES: Proportional to the amount of traffic that frequents the place, as always.
PREPARATION: Finding the right spot.
COST: The cost of entry.
PLEASURE: Antiquated, of course.
RISKS: The guards and the moldiness.
INCONVENIENCES: Dust/filth around the monuments that are rarely visited.

the lost city

"No one really visits this archeological site anymore, even the maps of the city hardly show it. Even so, when we arrived there we were terribly saddened to discover only a few rocks still standing to barely suggest the lost city that must have thrived at such an elevation, two thousand years ago. She decided to take advantage of the open air to perfect her tan in a picturesque spot. The sea was visible in the distance; the rocks there were large, flat, and smooth. She stretched out on one of them. She took off the full-length sarong that she used as a dress and exposed her breasts to the sun; she beckoned me to come be with her, and there was no mystery to what she really wanted. Still, I thought it was risky, seeing as someone might arrive at any moment.... She agreed to be quick and what she did worked. I was seated with one knee bent beside her, she leaned over me, pulled out my sex and sucked on it until I came in her mouth. After that, no longer able to pretend that I was afraid of getting caught by surprise, I lay on top of her, and we made love on the ancient rocks that truly seemed to be a special place for many others." — Nick

≈ *In the Wee Hours: The Cemetery*

"We often visit Père Lachaise. The lady lain down on the tomb, toward the North, behind the Wall of Fédérés. She is dark black, naked under her trench coat that she quickly flashes open. Look, the rock is all wet."

— Marie L., *L'Autre face* (The Other Side) by Pierre Bourgeade and Marie L.

Making love in a cemetery seems a practice that is as old as the world is. We won't even discuss necrophilia, but instead will simply consider getting naughty on a tomb or behind a mausoleum. It goes without saying that we discourage such things.

ch 5. Evening Parties

Erotic encounters, those that naturally end in bed, unfold over the course of the evening, when on a date, at a dance club, or at the cinema. But sometimes it can be very tempting to consummate this budding seduction right away. Or, in other words, it is tempting to jump each other's bones right away, there, on the spot. Pulling it off is a lot less easy.

◉ In a Restaurant This is one of the most frequent male fantasies: The lady slides under the table and engages in fellatio beneath the tablecloth.... In real life, getting it on in a restaurant is not an easy thing to do. That is, unless you are in a certain type of establishment—an erotic restaurant. These swinger establishments offer their clientele the opportunity to ravage each other during the meal.

at the café—a bistro in the 14th arondissement

> "This is a bar, a simple Parisian bistro where the register, blocking the view, allows, thanks to a corner-turn privacy wall, a blind spot (between the fireplace and a closed window); if you get low you

have the opportunity to do whatever you want to the lady sitting on a certain stool who is not wearing panties under her skirt. She turns away from the other patrons, and the bottom half of her body is sheltered from the barman's view by the register. I ask her to slide her stool up to me and keep her legs parted. The rest is my business."

— Esparbec, *Guide la Musardine du Paris sexy* (The La Musardine Guide to Sexy Paris)

At the Movies

"Classic" Cinema

At a move theater, lovemaking to conclusion, with penetration and orgasm for both partners, is a truly difficult challenge. The best position would be to have him seated and her sitting atop him, with her back to him. It is a must to pick an adult movie (one that is rated R). It is important that there is nobody around; on the other hand, possibilities still exist for mutual masturbation and fellatio. The hallway to the bathrooms is also a possibility. Avoid times when children's movies are showing. Those little monsters always want to go pee-pee during the movie.

At an X-Rated Movie

There aren't many real pornographic theaters left. X-rated movies are generally viewed in the home or on the sly in the back room of erotic movie rental and sales stores. Viewing booths have always been the seat of intense erotic activities, even if this is sometimes of a homosexual nature, and the private rooms in a straight porn theater are not exempt.

DIFFICULTY: Finding the right room/theater, the right seat, and the right film. Try to find something with dark cinematography so that there is little light in the room.

PREPARATION: Buy your ticket at the window.

COST: Just the tickets, $8–10 each. (You won't have to buy popcorn, which you would probably just knock over anyway.)

PLEASURE: Caresses and oral sex, in the best circumstances.

RISKS: Getting cornered by the manager. There are many ushers!

INCONVENIENCES: The seats rocking and closing on themselves as soon as you move—you could pinch something!

In a (Dance) Club

"Traditional" Nightclub

There's not much there except maybe the toilet stalls.

Swinger Club

Having sex with your lover in a sex club or a swinger club is a particularly amusing experience because it conjures up many feelings and multiple fantasies, from exhibitionism to the possibilities of playing out naughty fantasies you've always wanted to try in a nightclub (see "'Traditional' Nightclub," above), such as role playing with your partner as if you were strangers who have just met at a swinger club. The principal interest in these places is that "It is all set up for you."

Costume

Remember, Madam, partying at clubs is so extraordinary that all manner of dress is permitted. You can spend the whole night in a state of undress if you want. No one will reproach you for this, and the looks you get will not be strange! Everyone will enjoy the party so much the more. You might be surprised to discover that, even though you are baring it all, you still have to make the first move. It is for the best, and you will find it pleasing. Therefore, Madam, you get your pick and are free to choose the erotic situation you prefer.

It makes sense in some ways to allow open access to your little treasures without having to worry about mussing the delicate fabric of your cocktail dress. So party in the buff or with as little on as you dare wear. Just remember that you will need something to wear for the cab ride home. Many boutiques offer clothes designed for just this circumstance. Try any of the lingerie stores or stripper/adult-costume shops. If you are happy with your body image, you may be tempted to wear a pretty corset that is untied easily with the pull of a string. Dressed like this, the night belongs to you. Because of your outfit, he should choose underwear and pants that allow space for his erection and its easy release at the chosen moment, something that lets you pull him free without worrying about hurting him or the garment. Zippers risk roughing the delicate skin and pulling tangled short hairs, and no underwear gives better access than no underwear at all. What's more, in the right club, a man can walk around undressed just as well as a woman, enjoying the same privilege as is generally acceptable.

Please note that he is advised to carry condoms for the pleasures in which he is about to engage. And if he intends to engage in any oral stimulation, he may consider bringing along a dental dam as well.

≈ *Quick! Let's Go!*

Swingers' clubs were created to offer multiple possibilities to their clientele for having sex. The rooms and the furnishings—private booths, glory holes—are all intended to make things as comfortable and easy as possible. Basically, almost anything goes, or you can pleasure yourself and others with the objects at hand. Tables and barstools are fair game to play on here, where otherwise you could only imagine doing so.

≈ *Private Booths*

These are small rooms that often have a regular door you can close for privacy, or they can be left open for all passersby to see. They may be furnished with a bed that has a mattress covered in faux leather or something easily cleaned—you've probably seen something similar before. Most of the booths tickle the imagination with some decorative feature associated with the bed, like a mirrored ceiling or mirrored wall at the least. Some are fashioned with two-way glass that allows the voyeurism to extend to those not invited to participate directly, so that they can at least enjoy the spectacle if they so desire. Some booths are a sort of giant aquarium where the lovers are separated from the spectators by a large glass. Having sex in this sort of setup is a way of finding out for yourself if you have a taste for exhibitionism. More precisely, spending a few moments in a closed booth where your behavior is on display will either be a luxury you have always dreamed of—or not. The sounds emanating from the neighboring booths, the mirrors that show you at another angle—what a thrill! The only thing to keep in mind: good hygiene. Take a look around before you let loose and clean up any evidence left (by your) behind.

≈ *Darkrooms*
As their name indicates, in the darkness.

≈ *Beds*
Most clubs have larger beds in an open room where everyone can see what's going on. A king-sized four-post bed with room for six to eight people is a classic example. These may be canopied or mirrored from above, clad in exotic linens, mood-lit like a Rat Pack love nest, and piled with fluffy pillows to help make different positions more comfortable. This, too, is a place where you will learn your own preferences in regard to voyeurism and exhibitionism. Please note that it is perfectly acceptable for a couple to make love on "their side" of the bed or in the middle of a cluster of naked bodies without being obliged to share themselves with the others, beyond what they want.

Some clubs also have round beds, with mirrors above. Recently, when a contemporary artist tried to transform his show with an installation meant to evoke a bordello-like atmosphere, it was a round bed with red sheets that became his symbol; this object's presence alone created the desired effect.

≈ *Glory Hole*
This invention revolutionized the history of fellatio, or more exactly, it glorified the age-old practice of "the anonymous blowjob." A couple can easily take advantage of this device. It is only a matter of him placing his erect penis through an opening in a wall, without fear of being harmed by the edges of the hole, which is usually four inches in diameter or more. Because men are different heights—and different sizes!—there may be

several holes or something to stand on to accommodate different bodies. Take note; most of the time, he has the option of kneeling on a cushion or leaning against a padded wall. She will be on her knees on the other side of the divider. She can suck him and pretend he is anyone in the world or a total stranger—or maybe he is! How can you tell one penis from another in the dark? Can he recognize her mouth from that of another? No doubt whatever you decide will be unforgettable.

≈ *The Club Itself*

Having sex in a bar or on the dance floor is probably one of your many fantasies. Happily, in a swingers' club the rules of normal restraint are suspended!

The bar stools offer numerous possibilities. She can sit on one facing him with her legs spread wide—get rid of those panties if you haven't already. He can stand facing her and fill the empty space between them. She can swivel around to lean on the bar while lifting her pretty rump up off the seat, with a little arch in her back.... The stool is great for making all the standing positions easier and more comfortable with a twist.

The bench seating or booth tables at the clubs may have always fascinated you. Go ahead and play it out in the swinger's club; here you can enact what you've always dreamed of!

Even the dance floor can be more fun than usual. The metallic poles you often find there for striptease dances may inspire you to some provocative poses. They are just as good for steadying yourself or holding on when things get acrobatic. She might want to hang on with a firm grip while he jostles her from behind. You may notice that almost every swinger's club (and strip club) has a mirrored wall to reflect the imagery of the dancers and give the room a more vast and larger appearance. Whatever the reason, it also shows off your moves, whether you are dancing or doing something else.

The bathrooms in these clubs are also quite popular. In fact, many clubs are equipped with unisex showers. Sure, it is a lot like getting it on in your shower at home—except for all the people!

DIFFICULTIES: Getting up the nerve to go to a swinger club.

PREPARATION: Pay attention to the dress code for the club you choose. Otherwise, they might not let you in. The rest is just a matter of getting psyched-up for it. It is highly recommended that you choose a club or party that caters to couples.

COST: The cover charge; it is usually around $50 per couple.

PLEASURE: Total abandon. A voyage of discovery.

RISKS: Being grossed out or turned on: You may be totally into it, or you may be shocked by the vulgarity.

INCONVENIENCES: Being recognized at this kind of club or party by someone you know. But, hey, what is he or she doing there anyway?

≈ *Bathhouses*

Like swinger clubs, gay or mixed bathhouses are a destination for couples who want to have sex in public without being hassled. So what you find at these places is an environment meant to cater to those who enjoy sex and getting wet; there are rooms and lounges with bedding or lawn chairs and others with video screens showing pornographic movies. The saunas, Jacuzzis, and other pool areas are the only places where you are discouraged from having sex, because you might get heatstroke and because the proprietors would have to change the water more frequently.

mixed sauna

> "I once found myself [...] at a spa near Place Clichy, not completely finished partying; I was sunk into a winged-back chair, and there was an enormous bed next to me in the middle of the room. My head was at the right height to enjoy the spectacle before me; I could touch and taste the action of arms braced against the headboard while I pleasured a different sex with each hand. Their legs were high in the air and one by one, as their excitement reached a sufficient plateau, they each begged for attention to their ass."
> — Catherine Millet, *The Sexual Life of Catherine M.*

DIFFICULTIES: Getting the nerve up to go into a bathhouse.
PREPARATION: None. You don't even have to bathe; you will be washed while you are there.
COST: Somewhere around $40.
PLEASURE: Depends on the ambience.
RISKS: In some shady establishments, you will find creeps who wreck the vibe, gawkers....
INCONVENIENCES: Athlete's foot.

ch 6. On Vacation

Love on the run! The thrill of the journey plays a part in the pleasure.... We are going to take this in a direction that will reveal the erotic aspects of several modes of transport.

Ground Transportation Having sex in a car is a fantasy that is so well known that most people have already tried it. It is just too tempting and too easy. In the 1960s, many women lost their virginity in the backseat of a car. Luckily, Americans enjoyed large comfortable vehicles, unlike Italians who had to try to get it on in a Fiat 500.... According to Marion Alexandre, a psychiatrist in Paris, magazines like *Caradisiac* [equivalent to *Car & Driver*] suggest that "the car is nothing more than an extension of the driver and, in this way, reflects his personality and dreams. Psychiatrists take this even a step further: To them, the automobile is no less than an extension of the phallus."

SEDUCTION AND SCORING It is an eternal paradox—at least since the invention of the automobile—that the types of cars that grab the most attention and appear so seductive are impractical for "scoring." Do the sexy little sports cars that rip off the line—with their throaty rumbling engines, racing seats bolted low to the floorboard, and amazing acceleration—

remind you of anything like boys with toys? In the ideal setup, the couple wants to own a snazzy little sports coupe that brings the looks, but they also want to have a "family" car that lets them enjoy "the ride" in comfort. The only problem is deciding whether it is more fun to race around getting looks or steam up the windows at make-out point.

≈ *In a Parked Car*

The automobile naturally evokes different emotions depending on whether it is in motion or not, whether you are making use of the seats or the hood, whether you are satisfied with oral sex or you want to go all the way.... Making love in the car is a practice that is so integrated into our culture that every year there is at least one marketing campaign that plays on the ambiguities of a model name, like one manufacturer who launched a new minivan called the "Position." This vehicle, according to the imagery of the advertising, describes the many ways one can fold, adjust, and configure the six or eight seats that come with the vehicle, as well as the many ways its occupants can take advantage of these combinations.

Recommended Reading

Emmanuelle by Emmanuelle Arsan. New York: Grove Press, 1971.

Jean, the future spouse of Emmanuelle, takes them into the woods of Fontainbleau. The lady is still a virgin. "He had me lie across the bench seat, which had had its back reclined; I saw the green tops of the trees. Opening the door he was able to stand over me. In a moment he was inside of me. I came so hard I almost fainted...."

DIFFICULTIES: Finding the right car and the right place to park. You will probably have better luck in the countryside than in an urban setting.
PREPARATIONS: The usual stuff, or you can switch it up by taking out the seats.
COST: Gas.
RISKS: Getting busted for being naughty in your car.
INCONVENIENCES: The parking brake or stick shift prodding you in a soft spot.

≈ *In a Moving Car*

Engaging in the full act in a moving car is totally impossible and dangerous. Imagine causing a pile-up on the highway like the one caused by a couple in Germany. While she was blowing him, he lost control of the vehicle. He should be happy he didn't lose his penis in the incident; one bump in the road and your lover's teeth do the rest. On the other hand, those passengers in the backseat can do whatever they want so long as it doesn't interfere with the driver's ability to operate the auto. There are limousine companies that cater to the rock-star types, with full bars, plush seats, privacy glass, everything you could want for getting freaky on the road, including a retractable window between passengers and the driver.

on the road with catherine millet

> "He drove the convertible down the winding roadway to a parking spot overlooking Nice.... He put his hand over mine to guide the movements as I groped him through his jeans. [...] Then there was the fidgeting with his trousers and the minor

struggle to free his member, too big to fit through the cotton envelope at the front of his underwear. He had to use his own reach to finally bring all the goods out together. I was always nervous that I might hurt him. So, I let him help me. Now that I had good access I could stroke him properly. I never start off too quickly; I prefer to savor the full length of the experience, stretch tight the elastic skin of the tip. I put it in my mouth. My entire body moves to effect the greatest pleasure possible...." — Catherine Millet, *The Sexual Life of Catherine M.*

> ### *The Highway Patrol and Love on the Run*
> United States law varies state-by-state in forbidding certain practices that could impair the driver's ability to "perform." Most people find those highway patrolmen pretty hot—they are a common object of fantasy—but be careful about actually propositioning one, or you could find your women's prison dreams coming true.

on the way back from the beach

"We headed back from the beach as night fell. We were sitting in the back of a car driven by a friend of ours. He chatted with his girlfriend in the passenger seat. We quickly realized they were launching into a long discussion over the details of an event we did not attend. I lay my head on his lap and felt his sex on my cheek. I knew he was naked under the towel because I saw him take his trunks off earlier, wet and full of sand, so he could ride home at ease. I groped him a little but really I had other things in mind. I slipped my bikini bottoms down discreetly and repositioned myself in the seat so my legs could be slightly spread. He understood what I was doing right away, played with me all the way home, pressing his fingers deep within me several times and even tickling my little ass. I don't think I have come so hard and so many times in my entire life. From time to time, between spasms of pleasure where I had to bite my lip to keep quiet, I would glance at the road to see where we were and check that our friends in the front seat were still lost in their debate." — Julia

GARAGES AND PARKING LOTS The best! How many make-out stories are realized while parking? How romantic, how easy! In Italy, this type of interlude is practically written into their constitution. There are even organized advocates for keeping garages available for just that.

≈ *Love in a Car: Exhibitionism and Swapping*

The automobile is an essential element linked to these two practices. There are more than a few streets in the Paris area that are known for the naughty pleasures that can be had there. Couples arrive from all over the city to find a covered spot and take refuge there, windows rolled up, doors shut tight, and all kinds of kink within. Women are mostly undressed, and both partners enjoy themselves freely. Nearby, voyeurs, like moths to a flame, find the hottest action and masturbate themselves to exhaustion.

The cars are also integral to the ritual of swingers seeking each other out. Some places are very specifically known for this—with the efforts of a few promoters. Dozens of vehicles will cluster there to answer the call. It is practically an international phenomenon.

ON THE HIGHWAY At the end of 2003 the following report was issued from an agency: "A young couple, who were overwhelmed by lust, astounded motorists by making love in the middle of the night on the median of Highway A7 near Vaucluse [France]. After stopping their vehicle in the emergency lane, the young woman, 22 years old, and her companion, 24, climbed up on the barrier to the median close to the exit for Morières, where they passed a half an hour with the boy's feet dangling out into the highway's fast lane. Drivers called it in, and the highway patrol discovered the couple there, still wrapped around each other, and [the officers] took them to be held at the Morières jail. They're to be arraigned before the district attorney's office, and [they] are expected to be instructed as to basic highway safety and conduct."

THE CARS BEST "MADE FOR THAT"

Cherokee, Range Rover, etc. Luxury 4x4s have lots of interior space, making them an obvious choice for adventure inside the vehicle. Plus, you can drive them almost anywhere.

BMW family vehicles. These larger models have turned out to be better adapted for fun than anyone might have thought.

Minivans. The minivan is great for this kind of fun, and it doesn't matter who makes it. Since the invention of the Renault Espace, libertines on a mission have found this to be a favorite, whether in town or out in the countryside. Let's cite another article from our friends down at the weekly *Caradisiac*:

> "**For an evening of Karma Sutra, our crack staff overwhelmingly chose the Toyota RAV-4 as a getaway vehicle.** For those who like snuggling, the RAV-4 is perfect, thanks to its removable back seats. Without them there is more headroom, quite ideal [for lusty action]. Cecile liked the velvety upholstery for the seats but complained about the console. Julien noted that when the front seat backs were fully reclined, they fall into perfect alignment with the backseat bench.
>
> "**The Peugeot 206** was a pleasant surprise for everyone. It is much bigger than it appears—the seats upfront are the ones you want. Julian says, 'She is very roomy inside, and the reason is simple: The front seats (on the S16) are fixed low and are easily adjustable. Even in back, things are better than you might think; no doubts there's room for a backseat session!' The 206 is notably the smallest of our sample group."

≈ *Recreational Vehicles*
Campers and such. Ah, to daydream of retiring.

≈ *Vans and Delivery Trucks*
One is reminded of the scene in *The Tall Blond Man with One Black Shoe*, in which Jean Rochefort is convinced that his friend, played by Pierre Richard, is furrowing his wife in the back of a delivery truck. In actuality, the truck is filled with audio equipment that the thugs are using to spy on The Tall

Blond Man. Still, it is a pretty good idea! One of the great symbols of the hippie culture is perfectly suited for this eventuality. The van, generally an American-made truck of imposing dimensions, was chosen as a mode of expression and instrument of seduction by generations of playboys on wheels. The back of the van is usually equipped and decorated like one of Hugh Hefner's bedrooms. Mirrors line the walls or ceiling, the large mattress is covered in flannel and thick blankets, there is mood lighting or candles to go along with the quadraphonic sound system piping in intoxicating music, etc. Making love in this environment resonates especially with certain free thinkers, which is good because, in general, you have to borrow this kind of bunk from the owner. Or, you could rent it from him for a couple of hours....

Who knows? You might even get some decorating ideas for your place. The transformation of a van into a "love bus" opens your eyes to new horizons. For example, you can park your love bus overlooking an amazing vista, far out in the country or near the top of a mountain, far out somewhere that is isolated yet still accessible. In any case, it is a whole lot sexier than your parents' tow-behind.

DIFFICULTIES: Finding the right vehicle.
PREPARATION: Long months of planning and patching it together. Make sure it is worth the effort.
COST: The price of the vehicle and the expense of outfitting it.
PLEASURE: Perfect; unique; all the advantages of a good bed and all the fun of an amazing vacation.
RISKS: None.
INCONVENIENCES: The price of gas.

expert advice

> "The cabin of a tow-behind trailer is better in the long run; at least they have dedicated bunks."
> — Catherine Millet, *The Sexual Life of Catherine M.*

≈ Motorcycles

The motorcycle is a fantastic object—it makes my loins burn just thinking of being on one. Vroom! There are some other ways you can take advantage of it. Parked inside the garage, for example, it makes a fine substitute for a bench. She can lie back across it and become part of the ride. She can also mount it like a rodeo bull and buck and whoop and holler with her rump bouncing up and down while he sits just behind her in the saddle. Erotic imagery may play an important role in this situation, although there is no need to explain that these positions are not exactly comfortable or may even be dangerous. The bike can topple over and land on your leg, resulting in extreme discomfort.

≈ Completely Inappropriate Vehicles

The bicycle, even the tandem version, is a seriously bad choice of vehicle for lovemaking. It could quite possibly cost you any future thoughts of having sex again. Also, avoid the pogo-stick, skateboard, etc.

On the Water

≈ Boat

The cabins of steamships or ferryboats are particularly attractive for a night of erotic lovemaking. The bunks are often very narrow, which may make you feel a bit squeezed, but you will be safe from intrusion, together in a strange place, and the atmosphere we have been trying to recreate in these pages is there for enjoying.

There is only one inconvenience, but it is a big one: seasickness! You risk being miserable with your partner for the entire duration of the trip or may even get sick in the middle of a private moment. The medications that treat seasickness may make you drowsy, and there is almost no way to get complete relief. Pray it doesn't happen to you!

On a sailboat or yacht, the risk is the same, along with how wild the party can get if you are with the right group. This can turn into the time of your life if you have a taste for exhibitionism or trading partners. Making love in the bow of a sailboat is not without risks: You could get flipped into the water. Don't even mention the ropes!

DIFFICULTIES: Almost none, once you are onboard.
PREPARATIONS: Like packing for any vacation.
COST: The ticket for the trip.
PLEASURE: Novel; exotic.
RISKS: Drowning or being shipwrecked, but that is pretty rare.
INCONVENIENCES: Seasickness.

≈ *Rafts and Canoes*

Rafts and canoes provide limited shelter and safety but great romantic imagery. One classic scenario of having sex outdoors: making love on a raft tied to the shore near a waterfall.... The nineteenth century, the age of cannons and the quest for gold, has given us a good number of stories of romantic adventure achieved in such settings. It is a good idea to moor your craft properly, in a place certain not to be accessible from the river bank or visible from the river. The only way you can have sex in a small craft is lying down. You should plan to have at least a thick blanket or plush towel beneath you for cushion; she lies down, and he must achieve a balance with his motions. If the slightest bit of water starts to come over the gunwale, you risk being swamped.

A small skiff can serve just as well to transport you to isolated spots in nature where you are free to frolic openly, far from prying eyes. Don't forget to tie the mooring line properly. Consider a small beach, recessed from the rest of the coast, deserted and ignored, or a clearing only two steps from the river where it opens up to a deep gorge, far from daily strife, far from the rest of the world.... Any operation that runs small boat tours can give you more options.

DIFFICULTIES: None, if you know how to row.
PREPARATION: Fast.
COST: Launch fee at the marina.
PLEASURE: Amusing; scenic; retro.
RISKS: Drowning or sinking, but both are incredibly rare.
INCONVENIENCES: Mosquitoes.

◉ Public Transportation

≈ *Subways*

The subway is not a good choice for an adventure! It might work in the dead hours of the night, but, if so, we have no idea how.

≈ *Planes*

Making love undisturbed on a plane is not really possible unless you are flying to Canada, specifically to Whistler in the west. There, the Love-Air Company offers a short thirty-minute hop in a Cessna whose rear cabin is made up like a bedroom. For $250 Canadian, you can join the Mile High Club, if it even really exists, which is made up of people who claim to have had sex in mid-flight.

Otherwise, don't count on it. If anything, it is more likely you can get away with masturbating each other or perhaps enjoying some sneaky head, if you put a blanket over your lap on longer flights, and that too only if you have seats near the back of the plane. There's not much point in trying to get two people into one of the toilets, and the seats in coach are already becoming far too tight and uncomfortable for just one passenger, never mind two.

Recommended Reading

Emmanuelle by Emmanuelle Arsan. New York: Grove Press, 1971.

What we only dream of is realized by *Emmanuelle*: "Emmanuelle took a flight to London on her way to Bangkok." One of the other passengers in the first class section slipped into the seat next to hers and began touching her. After a few half-hearted rebuffs "…his hands managed to pry open a little space between her thighs: She was giving in." Following this beginning, "The man's fingers probed deeper and deeper into her soft, wet folds…" which leads Emmanuelle to take things into her own hands. The man guided her fingers "to wrap around his shaft and stroke in a special way so that her grip and technique were just the way he likes it."

DIFFICULTIES: Impossible, beyond a little fondling or mutual masturbation.

PREPARATION: Like getting ready for any flight, but naughtier.

COST: Prohibitive.

PLEASURE: Frustration is almost guaranteed.
RISKS: In the United States, at least twenty years in the cooler.
INCONVENIENCES: The same as on any flight, plus sexual frustration.

TRAINS Making love on a train is such a widely held fantasy that some very exclusive whorehouses offer a simulated train cabin, complete with optional vibrations and a conductor ("Tickets, please!") to complete the illusion of making love on a moving train and experiencing the risk of getting caught.

≈ *A Commuter Train*
Cancel all thought of it.

≈ *A Night Train*
If you have rented a compartment for an overnight rail trip to Venice or Rome, all the possibilities offered by this marvelous setting are yours to enjoy. Having sex in the bunk while trying to synchronize your movements with the undulating train is a pleasure that would make the gods and angels of sleep jealous. How could you resist exploring all the possibilities of this moving bedroom, especially those offered by the flip-down bed? She can sit up on it and have herself deliciously lapped by her partner who is kneeling down—just what they always dreamed of on the train ride together.

It is difficult to have secret sex on the train in one of the bench booths or wagon seating cars. Ideally, you might find one that is unoccupied or at least filled with blind people who are deaf and heavily drugged. That is, unless you are not opposed to getting it on in the presence of three or four shocked witnesses, or if it is perfectly dark and only the peepers pretending to sleep can catch a glance!

Sleeping cars are obviously a horse of a different color. The use of the narrow and slippery elevated planks, which are called sleepers by Amtrak and other international train lines, is obviously tempting a dark fate. Having sex on a train bunk is not very practical and depends on whether you use the lower bunk or the upper bunk. The bunk lower to the ground is barely wide enough for a person to lie on and nothing else; the one higher up only has enough clearance for you to wiggle into missionary position. But beware of turns of the track and the pitching of the train. The lower bench, when sat upon, offers all the same advantages as a chair or bench with a backrest and the added bonus of movement. She or he can keep one or both feet on the floor and stabilize themselves as they present whatever goodies they have to offer. Since they have the compartment all to themselves, the little stepladder that gives access to the upper bunks becomes invaluable. She can hold onto its rails and steady herself with it while her rump bounces around and he tries to line up and slip in from behind. He can also grab the rails of the ladder, with his back to the bunks, such that his sex is face-high to a standing partner and she can suck it. The movement of the train will no doubt remix the rhythm of this operation.

night train

"I met her on the train. I was coming back from the south of Spain with two fellow travelers I met at the Portuguese border. On the train from Madrid we clowned around with a group of young Germans. After hours of shooting the breeze, we went to search the train for empty cabins where we might be able to stretch out for a nap in peace. I tried to get her attention right away, and she went with me on our search. Something about her called to me: Her perky breasts had little pointed nipples that pressed through from under her shirt. I tried to hide my desire. I had no idea how I was going to convince her to let me caress them. We found an empty cabin in the next coach, she stretched out with her sleeping bag on one bench, and I did the same on the other facing her. I would probably still have been moping there if she hadn't come to join me. She was not prudish about preliminaries; she reached into my sleeping bag, found my sex, and started stroking me vigorously. I was worried I would jizz before I even had a chance to squeeze her titties! She seemed to know just how to play me though. She got on top of me in a straddle and, without even taking her panties off, just pulled them to the side so I could slip into her. The way the fabric rubbed me was a little rough, but I barely noticed: My fantasy was coming true; I was fondling the perkiest little pointed breasts, the sexiest I'd seen in my life. We came together as the train reached the next station. A few minutes later, our little cabin was overrun with loud passengers...." — André

DIFFICULTIES: Uncertainty.
PREPARATION: Buy your ticket; get to the station on time; etc.
COST: Ticket price.
PLEASURE: If all goes as planned, ecstasy is guaranteed! It is just like a dream come true.
RISKS: Biggest concern: the ticket taker and other passengers.
INCONVENIENCES: The train jolting or bucking unexpectedly; the questionable quality of the train cushions, ouchie!

ch 7. In the Countryside

> "**Agoraphilia** describes the desire to have sex in public places. Agoraphiles include those people who like to participate in sexual relations in their yard, a park, or any other outdoor place that gives them an especially exciting thrill."
> — *Dictionnaire des fantasmes et des perversions* (Dictionary of Fantasies and Perversions)

🌀 **L'Amour Outdoor** Having sex outside, in the open air, near the sea, in the woods, and even in green areas of the city is an intensely sensual experience.

All of the elements your body is exposed to can provoke unique sensations: fresh air, sunshine, the salty air of the ocean or mist of the river; the sandy beaches or mossy woods; the rumble of the city or the waves crashing on the coast; the smell of thyme, lavender, or hay; the prickle of the straw or the cool of unyielding stone; the humidity of a jungle or the chill of snow.

Making love outdoors is like inviting an invisible third partner to the party—the world around you. Nature, civilization, the whole universe—but don't forget about those who could stumble onto you. Always keep them in mind! Making love outside, for the more mystical among you, may even be a sensory experience that borders on the divine. Seriously. At its very essence, having sex outside is absolutely agreeable, terribly exciting, a new adventure, the first step toward countless possibilities and different sensations. Be open and creative and spice up your sex life. The same positions, caresses, and gestures take on a new meaning when your passion has you bent over a fallen tree trunk deep in the forest, stretched out on a warm sandy beach, or balanced on a rock high in the mountains.

Solemn Words of Caution

- No smoking after sex in the forest.
- Don't make the mistake of leaving your condoms at home.
- Don't disturb the flora, whether it is a bed of flowers or poison ivy.
- Don't disturb the wildlife—especially the wildlife that can harm you, such as a boar, bull moose, bear, etc.

THE PROPER ATTIRE Going out into the country is not the time to improvise. We're going to be having sex in many different places. Let's say that four out of five places we visit are not going to be good for our purposes: uncomfortable, too risky (you might get caught), or likely you'll be interrupted and have to get your clothes back on in a hurry. Picking an outfit that allows you to deal with all these challenges and circumstances elegantly is of great advantage. He should be well-dressed and wearing pants that open in the front easily; any underwear should be loose enough to accommodate his erection and allow him to easily present it. Consider that an erect penis bunched into tight briefs or restricted by an elastic waistband may be stifled or not perform as well. She should wear only dresses or skirts that are easily pulled up and that can quickly be pulled back down. Give up wearing underwear—what do you really need that for anyway? If you can't give up wearing underwear, try to wear something that can be pulled aside to allow for penetration without worrying that it will rub or pinch. Finally, remember that your clothes should also be durable, comfortable, and appear casual.

◎ A Trip to the Woods

THE COUNTRY CABIN The best scenario would be to own or rent a country cabin that is well protected and out of sight. Being protected from sight in the country is like trying to hide from KGB surveillance: Your safe house should be well hidden. Once you are tucked away there, everything is possible. A country home, reasonably furnished with rustic accoutrements, offers infinite pleasures to the outdoor enthusiast. Quick! Let's check out the place.

≈ *The Cellar*
"Visiting the cellar" is an age-old expression for performing cunnilingus or fellatio. So why not walk downstairs, literally, and "visit the cellar"? Now that could get interesting!

≈ *The Attic*
Dusty and perfectly charming, those old trunks haven't been used in a while. I bet you can use them for something.

IN THE GARDEN

≈ *The Seesaw and the Swing*

These are two inventions that have a rightfully important place in the history of erotica. The swing offers undeniable perks to sensual women. She, wearing a revealing skirt, sits upon it and throws her legs up toward the sky, revealing a little more skin each time she swings higher. Ideally, she is not wearing panties, and, as she swings, the air catches the fabric, pulling it back to reveal her thighs slightly parted, a fine spectacle for the smiling man before her. The *Dictionnaire de fantasmes et perversions* (Dictionary of Fantasies and Perversions) affirms that the swing will very quickly result in pleasure for the woman who uses it, "because of the friction and rocking motion that results from the vulva [resting] on the seat." Once her loins are warmed up from the swing, she will surely have an appetite for satisfaction.

For having sex, the swing is just the thing. She is seated. She has a firm grip on the rope at either side and is pulling her legs up and spreading them wide—or she can place her feet on the swing. He, standing in front of her (but at a safe distance), has a full-access view. A gentle rocking follows soon after her swing comes to rest. She can also lean way back on the swing so that she can place her ankles on his shoulders, which he takes hold of to keep her balanced. It is also possible for her to kneel on the swing, once again with a firm grip on the support lines. He takes her from behind by grabbing her hips. The effort to keep balance does the rest.

The seesaw offers many of the same advantages as the swing—and solid comfort, too. The two lovers can have sex in almost all the same positions as on a bed, with the added bonus of the sensations offered by trying to balance on the seesaw.

A Nearly Impossible Scenario: A group of Japanese flying trapeze artists have come to town. A man and a woman are on individual swings, facing one another, and they are trying to join with each other when their swings meet in mid-air.

DIFFICULTY: You have to get the hang of the balance and rhythm dictated by the swing.
PREPARATION: When you get the chance, don't miss it.
COST: Nothing.
PLEASURE: Thrilling; acrobatic; nostalgic.
RISKS: Falling.
INCONVENIENCES: Rough rope or twisted lines.

Recommended Viewing

Behind the Green Door by Jim and Artie Mitchell. Jartech, 1972.

Amateur swing lovers have their own clique! *Behind the Green Door* had a scene that made such an impression that they try to copy it to this day—a procession of couples, men and women, swinging with each other.

≈ The Barn

"Lying in the hay
With the sun on your face
A little bird sings far away
The three little words said
And the grand promises made
Like so many twigs in our hair
Kisses we share and the thrill
Ah! how life is so sweet, sweet
Lying in the hay with the sun on your face."
[...]

When one is full of life, full of love and many years
Not much else really matters
I don't care about the sheets
I won't be trapped by the bed
I will gather and savor sweet thrills."
— Mireille and Jean Nohain, *Couchés dans le foin* (Lying in the Hay)

Well, now that we know, we simply must go for a roll in the hay.

The barn has always been the perfect spot to play out your country lust. Lying in the hay, having a tumble with a farm girl, or getting laid by a ranch hand are parts of a fantasy near and dear to some people. For the whole thing to go well, it is important that it happens naturally. It is a good idea not to mention it in advance. Instead, simply take your partner by the hand and lead him/her to a pile of golden straw. There, tear each other's clothes open, just enough for sex, and have fun; she, with her breasts bouncing above the rim of her corset, or he with his pants at his ankles and his cheeks in the hay.

But wait just a second: You should also beware. The first thing to do is make sure there is no pitchfork in the hay. That could be really bad. Also, this is not a good adventure if either of you has allergies. Hay fever, as its name indicates, is not a joke. Finally, the straw—hay that is dry and brittle—pokes you in the butt, but that can be part of the adventure.

Unfortunately, good, old, big country barns are growing more and more scarce. Storing hay or straw in large warehouses or under plastic tarps is depriving us of one of our more historic delights.

DIFFICULTY: Refer to the above.
PREPARATION: Find a barn. If the coast is clear, go.
COST: None.

PLEASURE: Nostalgic and a sure bet.
RISKS: Danger! No smoking.
INCONVENIENCES: Hay fever; skin irritation.

≈ *The Stables*

Not recommended if still in use. The smell is enough to kill the mood. Still, there might be a mule or two that would be to Lady Chatterley's liking. Otherwise, all feed storage areas and animal shelters on a large farm can be used, as there is always a wall to lean against or a barrel you can step up on or a sack of something—apples, grain—that you can lie upon. Whatever it is, though, you'll probably get dirty rolling around on it.

≈ *Streams and Meadows*

A lush meadow, full of tall reeds to hide in, is dreamy. A party that ends with your feet up in the air starts out just like a picnic. First, remember to spread a blanket on the ground to protect your delicate skin from pest and prickle.

Don't ignore the trails and streams or the farm equipment strewn about. You can have a lot of fun with a wheelbarrow! She can sit back with her legs on the outside of the handles while he occupies the space between them. The drawings illustrated by l'Aretin present an improbable configuration: The woman holds onto a handle on either side of a wheel, and the man, seizing her legs firmly, penetrates her while carrying forward, in effect making her a living wheelbarrow.

AT THE FARM, WE ALL HAVE SEX LIKE ANIMALS The *Kama Sutra* teaches us what is involved in the Congress of a Cow: "When a woman is bent over with her hands and feet touching the ground like a quadruped, and her lover mounts her from behind like a bull, it is called the 'Congress of a Cow.'

At this time, everything that is ordinarily done on the bosom should be done on the back." Each type of animal copulates differently, so you are encouraged to imitate the subtle differences in technique.

≈ *In Nature's Glory*

Making love outside, in the country, sharpens the senses. This is so because, among other things, one must consider what other animals will be in the surroundings, whether different species of animals or humans—drifters, campers, farmers, and field hands. The most dangerous of all these is the hunter who may not be able to distinguish at a distance between "the beast with two backs" and large game.

In sum, you have to be discreet and yet remain aware of what you can and cannot see!

DIFFICULTY: Depends on how close you are to animals and other humans.

PREPARATION: When the moment arrives, go for it.

COST: Free, for the most part.

PLEASURE: Nostalgic; natural.

RISKS: Check local legal codes. Stay away from brambles and thorny vegetation or anything that could cause a rash, like poison oak. Check hunting seasons for your region. Pay attention to animal life, giving special attention to young bulls or protective mothers of any species.

INCONVENIENCES: Hay fever; skin irritation.

the equipment shed

"Sunday afternoons at my parents' home are always capped off with a long nap in front of the TV after supper. We left them snoozing to go for a walk around their property, situated on the outskirts of a southern town. The trails went up the hill, and we knew them all well, but this time we took a small detour on a forest path and stumbled onto what looked like a little cabin, half filled with tools and junk. Right away we got the idea to have some fun there. I'd already slid my hand halfway down her pants as she pulled off her T-shirt, freeing her breasts…. Then all at once the stink was overwhelming! It was a very small skunk that appeared from under the cobwebs on an old pile of tools, and what a stink! We ducked out in a hurry, sheepish and ready to get away from there all together! But a few steps around the building and away from the skunk we decided that we shouldn't waste our chance after all. So she pressed through a squeaky door on the other side of the cabin and took her panties off. We had sex standing up in a quiet corner of the country property. It was quiet before we got there, at least! I will always remember the noise of the squeaky door and the way it clacked against the old metal rung each time her ass nudged against it." — Seth

◉ **Some Rural Areas to Do It** Rather than suggesting particular areas, we invite you, the reader, to send us descriptions of your best outdoor lovemaking experiences that you might want others to experience, along with any special advantages and inconveniences or warnings for people who want to check your suggestions out. E-mail your ideas to

DoingItNaturally@hunterhouse.com. We'll share some of the best e-mails we receive with other readers and on our website. Let's see if we can't put together a fun guide to making love outdoors in the USA!

the river

"We walked around in the Perigord area [in France] searching for a river of fresh water to bathe in. We found a trail that would lead us to a branch of the Lot River. After walking a few hundred yards, we found a little patch of pebble rock beach where we put our camping chairs and things. It was impossible to go swimming, though, because from one side to the other and for as far as we looked, the water was no more than a foot deep, so we went back to the little beach where we were set up close to a copse. We put our towels and our clothes over the chairs to screen us—not very well—from anyone wandering through, and we made love on the wet, lumpy ground. After we exhausted the few positions sustainable on such an uncomfortable surface, I got up to sit on one of the chairs, naked, rod in the air, and she came and sat on my lap facing away from me. It was the best; I could have stayed there with her forever, the soft breeze… the great outdoors!" — John

❂ **In the Forest** The tree is your best friend for a romp in the forest. Trees serve as towers that you can hide behind and lean on for different kinds of frolicking.

the forest at fontainebleau

"We planned to hike out across the forest at Fontainebleau, from one side to the other. We ran into groups of people also drifting through, and looked around a few picnic spots.... Several times, we decided to look for the perfect place to lie down for a while. It was cool out, and the weather was dry, but everywhere there were piles of moist leaves too wet to roll around in. So, we redirected our hike toward the deepest part of the woods and decided to look for the right tree. We wanted it to be completely hidden from view, with low-slung branches that would be great for lounging upon, dry if possible...and we found it. It was perfect, just like we imagined it would be, a large fallen tree that was propped up by another fallen trunk lying on the ground. She pulled her pants down to her ankles and bent at the waist to lie front down across the wood; I slid in behind her and, standing, penetrated her.... It was superb! And so discreet! Then a few minutes later, while getting "restarted" in another position, we discovered that each one of our movements shook the branches of the tree, the one it was leaning on, and others that were touching it. Let's just say that the entire forest could make out our location from the way we were shaking the branches in what we thought was a secret little spot." — Adam

≈ The Trees

There are many ways a tree can serve your needs when frolicking outdoors. It is great to lean against in many ways, depending on the position you've chosen, and you might be amazed at how many different uses you can find for a low branch protruding from a thick trunk. Each time you find one, it inspires your creative desires. The *Kama Sutra* even has a position called the Tree: "The man is standing up. Facing him, the woman puts one foot on his and lifts her thigh as high as her partner's pelvis, which makes penetration easier." Perfect for the woodlands.

A tree can inspire fantasies that are easy to role-play—for example, a damsel in distress or a man tied up and left for the cougars. Just tie your partner (superficially) to a nice tree, either nude or with clothes torn open.... It is up to you to make up the rest. You can pretend to offer your victim as a sacrifice, tear off his or her lower garments, or quite the opposite... allow yourself to be tamed and succumb to your captor's caresses. Remember to keep the noise down if you don't want to attract the attention of others and—whatever you do—don't abandon your partner in a vulnerable position!

DIFFICULTIES: Finding a wooded area with enough privacy.
PREPARATION: Don't forget adequate protection.
COST: Nothing, unless you get caught.
PLEASURE: Sublime. When everything goes well, sex in the woods is a delicacy.
RISKS: Wild animals, hunters, hikers.
INCONVENIENCES: Various pests.

≈ *The Bed of Dried Leaves*

You don't always have the bare necessities—a mattress and blanket—with you, so you may want to take advantage of the natural resources at hand. A bed of dry leaves is pretty easy to put together in early autumn, after the leaves have begun to fall and before the rains leave them soggy. Gather dry leaves and make a pile about six feet long. The weight of a couple rolling around will quickly compress them into a mat. Remember to pick a place hidden from view and check the ground for jagged rocks or exposed roots that can poke you. One of the partners—the chivalrous gentleman, of course—improves the site by offering an article of clothing to lie on. No problem, that's what laundry is for. It will no doubt be he who lies on the brittle mass, risking scratches on his back while she straddles him from on top. Still, a good bed of leaves offers nearly the same options as a regular bed. After you get up you can see the evidence of your rustling around and view all the poor leaves reduced to confetti and scattered around among the brush.

Be careful not to leave anything behind when you leave: wedding bands, used condoms, or anything else the animals can't use.

Recommended Viewing

The delicious Brigitte Lahaie, having sex in the forest, lying next to her horse, in *Je suis à prendre* (I'm Yours to Take) by Francis Leroi. Films du Palais Royal, 1976.

≈ *Unrealistically: On Horseback*

Fairy tales and ancient lore provide the imagery and descriptions of erotic couples having sex while riding a horse. Only a few circus-trained horseback acrobats might be able to attempt something like what is described in A. S. Lagail's *Les paradis charnels* (Carnal Delights), which suggests a stunt where "The acrobatic cavalier lies atop the steed's back facing upward. His lovely damsel facing him from above wraps her form around his as the pace of the horse quickens...." Even if the position were possible, how could the horse be spurred to the right gait? The passage goes on: "Its movements synchronizing with the in-and-out rhythm of the lovers in a wide open canter." Applying a little poetic license, we might even describe this act as the "taming of a noble beast."

ch 8. At the Beach or in the Mountains

There are times when you just *have* to get away! Making love out in the natural world is almost required. Be careful! The beach and the mountains get crowded. There may be a cluster of tourists armed with binoculars behind every rock, the lifeguards survey the dunes, kids are everywhere. You're never really alone.

At the Seaside A vacation at the beach cries out for adventurous sexuality: the warm weather, the sultry smell of coconut oil and sweat, all that young skin in the sun. While many beachgoers only think about the practical aspects of being in the heat, maybe you can let your imagination wander freely and create opportunities for special fun in the sand.

CREATE A BEACH KIT Going to the beach with every intention of misbehaving requires a little planning and some supplies. Unequivocally, the best situation would be to find a beach that is completely deserted. In the off-season, it is not that hard to find such a patch of sand, but to really get the most out of it you have to leave civilization behind. Anticipate the bare necessities or plan something slightly more refined.

You will need a large, thick, soft towel to lie on. Bring another that is just for drying off. Grab some handy wipes to assure the hygiene of your tender sex organs, sun block so that your genitals don't get burned, and beverages that keep you from becoming dehydrated.

While shopping, notice that there are shade tents on the market called "beach shelters" that are an excellent substitute for the unwieldy umbrella. Some of these even zip closed like a tent and allow you to escape the view of others. It goes without saying that a couple might dive into one of these when he gives the signal—something along the lines of a protruding bulge—as a wave of knowing eyebrows show the curiosity of those in proximity, especially if there are groans and a frantic ruckus emanating from within.

ON THE SAND Making love on the beach basically became the top fantasy of French men and women after the release of the 1957 film *And God Created Woman*, in which Brigitte Bardot and Jean-Louis Trintignant wrestle on the sand in St. Tropez. Let's just say it is, without a doubt, one of the easiest fantasies for a couple to fulfill. All you need is to find the right beach and the right moment. We've already said it will be much easier to get away with it in the off-season—between April and May or between September and October—rather than on beaches that are usually very busy, even at night, during the summer. During either day or night in a place far from waterfront residences, you can choose a spot situated between the dunes or tucked in the brush where you can make a quick exit if there is any problem. All the same, you should have a towel or some clothes handy to cover up evidence of your doings—his erection or her protruding nipples!

The most important thing, after you find a hiding place, is to avoid grit! Always spread out a thick towel on the ground. The sand is—as you no doubt already know—made of millions of particles of the hardest rocks. The sand will inconveniently stick to your skin, wet or dry. If his sex organ, moistened by her state of arousal, comes into contact with grit, the grit will stick to it tenaciously and render any attempt at penetration hurtful for both partners. In the parlance of amateur enthusiasts of sex "outdoors," it will be like rubbing with sandpaper. A sandy penetration of either the vagina or anus, with or without lubricant, with or without a condom, will be equivalent to corporal punishment. What's more, it is best not to get sand on your hands either, as it becomes difficult not to transfer it to your partner while fondling him or her. Then there are the mosquitoes!

Lovemaking on the beach is often classic: missionary unhurried, drowsy doggie, relaxed oral sex…. Anything is possible when you are in love.

at the beach

"It was a weekend near the end of June. Some idiot directed us toward a private beach west of Saintes-Maries-de-la-Mer where we would be able to camp undisturbed (but the whole world knew, except for us and the idiot, that the beach we were looking for was actually to the east of town). Long story short, after hours of walking through the tidal marshes, we found a place to sleep huddled in our sleeping bags close to the water's edge. In the morning, the sunrise was spectacular and that turned both of us on. We made love

> on top of our sleeping bags, then rolling around on the sand. Soon afterward, I noticed the sand sticking to her thighs and the wincing expression that followed, which was evidence of her burning discomfort. A few minutes later when she was coming back from rinsing off in the water, we saw a dozen or so horseback riders, tourists galloping through the park. They waved to us, so we figured they knew exactly what was going on." — Paul

Before you go out to shake it up on the sand, you should carefully choose the kind of beach you might like to roll around on. There are four types to consider, each having its own advantages and disadvantages.

FAMILY (PUBLIC) BEACHES This beach is just what you might expect. Making love there in the middle of the day would be pure folly. And these fine spots continue to be frequented by all sorts of people into the evening and beyond: stargazers, fishermen, skinny-dippers—like you.

NUDE BEACHES Especially in Europe, there are many of these beaches—the kind on which you can "camp" or sunbathe in the buff—like the Ile du Levant or the Montalivet, or the undesignated beaches left for you to explore on your own. The designated nude beaches don't particularly encourage you to treat them like a cheap hotel. Therefore, these places are not predictably permissive of "free love," unlike the beaches referred to as "liberated."

"LIBERATED" BEACHES If there are in fact nude beaches that are known as "liberated," they are obviously not officially known as swinger friendly. So don't make that mistake. All sexual activity that takes place in the open is subject to criminal prosecution. It is sad, but it is certainly true! Be wary of any sexual activity or the suggestion of it at such a place: The police will probably get interested very quickly in shutting it down and hauling away whomever they find involved in hanky-panky.

the beaches of cap d'agde, france, as seen by michel houellebecq

In **The Elementary Particles**, the book that proved his talent, writer Michel Houellebecq has already largely described the charms of these unusual spa waters, considered to be the Mecca of partner swapping by thousands of European libertines. The beach, scrutinized by the police, is described at length by one of the characters of this novel: "More than three kilometers in length, the nudist beach at Cap d'Agde slopes gently down; it is this that allows for leisurely bathing, even for young children. Its greatest section is reserved for public use and beach recreation (windsurfing, badminton, kite-surfing). It is unspoken but understood…that couples searching for an unconventional sexual experience should direct themselves toward the eastern end of the beach, a little above the Marseillan springs. […] Around two hundred couples would gather there in a restricted area. Several solo men could be seen wedged between the couples; others skirted the line of dunes, looking out in both directions."

"GAY" BEACHES There are no signs that read, "CAUTION: Gay Beach Next 500 Meters," but certain stretches of sand are almost exclusively visited by homosexuals. If this type of beach experience is not your desire, you will want to take note right away as to whether the frolicking nudes are of only one gender and then steer clear or dive in as you wish.

≈ *In the Dunes*
Warning, for those adventurers who aren't so concerned with the future of the environment: The flora of the dunes is extremely important and extremely fragile. Show respect for this fact, and do not trample or decimate the wild plants just because you have a burning desire in your loins. What's more, the flora can be prickly! Having sex in the dunes is very similar to having sex on the beach. The only difference is that you are a little less likely to be seen. Be careful nonetheless. The dunes that border the beaches that are known somewhat for their availability to sexual free-thinkers are a favorite haunt for perverts and voyeurs.

DIFFICULTIES: Finding the right time and right place.
PREPARATION: Spread your towel on the sand, take off your underwear, and bingo!
COST: Nil.
PLEASURE: Perfect, like realizing a childhood dream.
RISKS: Check local legal codes.
INCONVENIENCES: The sand; possible sunburn; other beachgoers.

≈ *In the Water*
There's something you should consider before having sex in the ocean. Women's natural vaginal lubricating juices dissolve in seawater, and there is no chance that you can take relief from artificial lubes because they dissolve just as quickly. The

answer then is to be speedy: Get in there while the mood has you hot and ready and know that toward the end things will not stay slippery. The use of a condom is almost impossible, as the water instantly washes off the lubricant, and you risk the rubber sliding off inside her. The female condom is a maybe. Men: Don't forget that it may be difficult to stay erect in cold water. It is known that when one's balls are freezing they retract into the body (please excuse this vulgar commentary!).

One of the major concerns for those considering water sports is the terrible rumor: In the water, you could get stuck, the effect of suction and clenching muscles prevents him from being able to withdraw from her. There is no proof of this; even if it could happen, the stress of the situation might cause him to soften or go limp enough so that the problem would solve itself. Still, you have to try it!

No one position is better than any of the others. He should plant his feet firmly on the seabed, be it rocks or sand. She can then wrap her legs around his waist and envelop his sex, allowing her buoyancy and the motion of the waves to do the rest. There is nothing for him to do but seize her by the waist and wiggle his hips (there is no need to use much of an in-and-out motion).

Unless you can hold your breath like a skin diver and you have the swimming agility of an eel, it is difficult to imagine a successful fellatio or cunnilingus. And yet, there is no reason not to give it your best effort. The memory of your attempt will make you grin ever after.

There is a pornographic film titled *Scuba Sex* that opened our eyes to new possibilities. The actors and their counterparts were equipped with weighted belts, like those worn by divers, which allowed them to move around more easily.

Underwater masturbation, however, has a great chance of coming off successfully. But you should know that the jet of sperm will float to the surface of the water around you and linger until the waves carry it away… if the waves carry it away at all. You should wash yourself carefully afterward in any case. Seawater is subject to different bacteria levels, and you could find it infiltrates your folds and creases.

DIFFICULTY: Finding the right time and finding a private place or a place that is an adequate distance from the beach.

PREPARATION: Get it while you can.

COST: A vacation to the beach; it could be expensive.

PLEASURE: Most of the time, it is not what you hoped for. But if you get lucky, it can be very agreeable.

RISKS: Almost none.

INCONVENIENCES: The water defeats the slipperiness, as mentioned.

Some of the Best Beaches

The best, the best! What is the best? Let's just say that these beaches are a good bet in the off season, when the lifeguards are not on duty and the beach is not covered in people.

Florida
- Sandestin Beach (Destin)—twenty-six miles of beautiful, white sand
- Bahia Honda State Park (Big Pine Key)—virtually uninhabited
- St. Joseph Peninsula State Park (Port St. Joe)—sand dunes, tall grass, white sand

Hawaii
- Ewa Beach (Oahu)—"Ewa" means "stray"; fewer tourists and people than other nearby beaches

- Lumahai Beach (Kauai)—unsafe for swimming and surfing, so there aren't many people around; freshwater stream to the left of the beach

California
- Black's Beach (San Diego)—naturist beach
- Baker Beach (San Francisco)—sand dunes provide protection from other people, but beach still offers gorgeous water views
- Enderts Beach (Crescent City)—very uninhabited, access to redwood forest and ocean views, can catch a glimpse of whales in the Spring

East Coast
- Chapoquoit Beach (Falmouth, MA)—tucked away from major roads, so there aren't many people around
- Oracoke Island (Hyde County, NC)—remote island, sand dunes, salt marshes, and light houses

If you have suggestions for beaches to add to this list, e-mail them to DoingItNaturally@hunterhouse.com. We'll share some of the best e-mails we receive with other readers and on our website.

◉ On Vacation There's more than just the beach. A little inland, there are just as many possibilities for relaxing and frolicking. You should always know how to take advantage of your surroundings.

≈ *Hammock*
The hammock is good for numerous erotic games. The two partners can lie side by side—the position that is easiest to enjoy is spooning—and she offers her rump to him. He moves

slowly in and out at first, but as the thrusts become more vigorous, the hammock will swing you higher and higher.

The charming quality of free suspension is similar to a sling, giving these "booty swings," as they are known in the jargon of gays, their name. She can lie on her back, perpendicular to the length of the hammock, and use her hands to hold her own legs spread wide, feet up in the air. While she is in this position, he penetrates her, rocks her, and bounces her bottom. She can also bend over at the waist, leaning her torso on the hammock. In this position, her feet can rest, touching the ground, or she can lift them and kick at the ground for a rhythmic rebound. He stands behind her, penetrating her, enjoying her bounce.

He can also lie back in the hammock on a beautiful summer day and lazily enjoy the perfect blowjob, or he can kneel below the hammock and offer cunnilingus to her as she stretches languidly across it. Alternatively, she can very delicately balance herself over him in such a way that his penis slides effortlessly between her lips.

DIFFICULTY: Tremendous or insignificant depending on what you try.
PREPARATION: Find two solid uprights for tying up the hammock.
COST: The price of the hammock.
PLEASURE: Leisurely or acrobatic.
RISKS: Falling.
INCONVENIENCES: Motion sickness.

≈ *Private Pool*
Making love poolside is a divine pleasure that is available to anyone who has access to a private pool and enough time to

take advantage of it. All of the positions you can imagine for having sex in the water or at the edge of the pool are possible. A soft towel is just about all you need to get it on in the sunshine and enjoy all the variations of a porn star's repertoire.

The pool itself opens the door for new ideas. She could lean her back to the pool wall, floating in the water and be taken standing up. Or, seated at the edge in the shallows, she can spread her legs and take him between them. He can sit on the edge of the pool while she floats in the water bobbing her head for his pleasure. The diving board has many uses as well. Have sex in the water and make use of the steps, handrails, and ladders—also quite agreeable. Don't forget the features of the pool's edge, particularly the spillway and jets that entice unedited creativity.

In short, how perfect is this pleasurable option for amorous activity? All you need is a pool, preferably one that is shielded from view.

DIFFICULTY: None.

PREPARATION: Find the pool.

COST: The pool, unless you have access to a friend's or neighbor's.

PLEASURE: Perfect.

RISKS: Falling into the water during a poolside or diving-board romp. Condom-in-water difficulties (see our earlier cautions, pages 105 to 106).

INCONVENIENCES: Chlorine!

≋ *Love with a View*

Having sex outside, in the open or on the balcony, in a place surrounded by beautiful landscapes, is a particularly enjoyable way to appreciate the view. It is one of the biggest reasons that making love on the beach is a principle fantasy for so many men and women.

So be picky about choosing the surroundings you want to be in but don't lose sight of the real reason you are going there—to satisfy your natural desires. A picturesque rock hollow near the edge of the sea, lashed by the waves, will give your seduction a marine flavor. A hike through the mountains or a lush valley stretches the imagination toward the infinite and gives you the impression of being on top of the world or far removed from daily concerns. In any case, don't forget a blanket; the rocks, sand, or meadows each have irritants that you should defend against. The rest is a matter of circumstances, and the timing for an opportunity can sneak up on you. A little walk down a country path leads you to a place where you won't be disturbed. The top of a hill, a cliffside, a marine cove—all can be just the place. What's important is knowing how to seize the opportunity when it comes along.

Yet even a simple little hotel room can awaken fantastic emotions if its window opens up to an impressive view. Research hotels with a broad view of the coast or the mountains and make love with the window open or on the balcony. Some buildings in particular, like the Marriott in New York, offer the impression of enjoying your romance on the roof of the world.

≈ *Camping*
For most couples, making love in a tent evokes memories of adolescent vacations or their first sexual explorations. It is not about comfort; having sex while camping is more rugged.

Everything takes on a new hue when the only rules are self-imposed. Modern tents are lightweight, easy to pitch, and made from opaque fabrics. They're easily stored in the trunk of the car or carried in a bag to almost any location. Let's take, for example, a small igloo tent, chosen only because it is lightweight. You don't need a fancy summer home; you just need a shelter where you can get naked and be out of view in the most extravagant places. Then, in the worst-case scenario, the only thing you can be accused of is having set up a tent on the bank of the river or in a clearing for a few minutes. The important thing is to avoid mixing exhibitionism with camping in the wild by brandishing your sexuality on a well-traveled trail or stumbling out of your tent naked, still moist from sex, hoping for a cigarette but finding a Boy Scout troop standing frozen, staring at you in disbelief.

A sleeping bag or a sheet is all you need besides the tent, and that's more for the convenience of cleanup than for comfort. One way you can start having fun with your tent right away is to pitch it at your house, near the sliding door or in the living room, so that you can verify for yourself just what you can do in it. There's almost nothing you can't do, except have sex standing up in it, of course!

DIFFICULTY: Finding a campsite.

PREPARATION: Pitching the tent. These days it takes about two minutes.

COST: Around $50 for the tent.

PLEASURE: All but assured.

RISKS: Being heard if you get too loud! Otherwise, practically none.

INCONVENIENCES: Packing up the tent when you are done.

the tent

"That summer, which we spent going from one campsite to the next across Southern Europe, our goal was to systematically make love everywhere we went with the tent flaps open to the fresh air. It was not a quest for exhibitionism; we did not want anyone to see us, but the tent we had turned into a sauna as soon as you got in it and started moving around a little. I remember her going down on me as I looked out at the water. I was seated halfway inside the tent, which we had pitched on the beach. At dusk, she came and sat down in front of me, naked, and started stroking me; I wanted to cum so bad it was like thunder struck with my orgasm…. Another evening, when our tent was planted on the highest clearing of a terraced campground, shadowed by tall trees, she got down on all fours, head poking out of the tent, while I slid all the way into her from behind. What must the other campers think of this girl with her head out in the fresh air, no top to be seen, rocking back and forth gently? Another time, it was my turn to hang halfway out of the tent. I was lying on a sleeping bag with my lower half inside the tent and the flap open. There was no one in sight because we set up the tent to open toward a rock wall that enclosed the site. She, straddling me inside the tent, wiggled gently. I was filled with the dark breath of a man inhaling the night.…" — Mike

In the Mountains

≈ *Among the Rocks*

A drive into the foothills is a sure temptation for two lovers who want to be intimate. With trails that lead to thickets and cloistered groves at every turn, caves and rock formations where it seems like it would be very easy to disappear.... The mountains, more deserted than the countryside, especially in the spring, have much to offer. But there are dangers as well! Keep your eyes open! Watch out for rockslides if you are near cliffs. Also, watch for animals attracted to your coupling and hunters or mountain climbers passing by, etc. Otherwise, the dynamics are very much the same as in the countryside, but in this case on a slope. Do remember that it gets cold! Strip down for a romp in the snow—why not?—but beware of frost to sensitive body parts (especially your genitalia) that are not accustomed to such temperatures.

---
love in the mountains

"We parked our car in the lot at the foot of the rising Grande-Chartreuse. We started wandering lazily forward on a little hike only a few hundred yards up the trail, but we never went any farther than that. There was a rock hollow, which we found too tempting, that ran under the length of a carved shelf like some kind of natural terrace. Laying down flat on our stomachs we could see the fertile valley below, the parking lot and our car sitting there all alone, not another person in sight. He made the first move, and I seized upon it! He had undressed himself completely as it was always a fantasy of his to be "buck naked in the natural elements." I had my buttocks on a rough and wet rock, but it was so cold it didn't hurt. Until later! After, I remember him wiping off both of our sexes with his briefs and for the rest of the trip, he was freezing his butt off under his jeans." — Lisa

≈ Campgrounds or Parks

If the campground or park is abandoned, you are in luck! The night belongs to you. If not, you can count on tiptoeing around in the usual way couples do when trying to make love in a public place. How about zipping your sleeping bags together and spending the night keeping each other warm? Then, anything goes as long as you are mostly quiet. In campgrounds these days, there always seems to be somebody shuffling around, though: climbers who break camp at two in the morning for an assault on the summit, yahoos who drink beer and make noise into the middle of the night, other couples who are trying to do the same thing you are. It seems like you can never really get away from it all.

≈ Snow and Igloo

Ideally, you can find a spot that is far enough away from other people but still accessible, so that you can build a decent little igloo. The way it is done, at least the way the experts describe it, is simple enough. Begin by carving out a circular hole in the snow. This should be possible unless the ground is frozen hard. The snow you dig out will be used to make the snow bricks, compressing a pile to a rectangular brick shape about 28 x 16 x 10 inches. Line the outside of the circle with a layer of snow bricks and spiral upward as you add more layers, inclining the bricks slightly toward the center of the circle. At the top, fit the final brick snugly into the opening. Finally, carve an entrance to the igloo, digging it half into the ground and half into the wall.

That's good enough for now; we'll leave the rest to be reinvented by the more adventurous among you. All the same, the reports and articles from naturalist clubs regularly extol the virtues of extreme sports, like hiking or trail skiing, in the nude. You gotta see it!

DIFFICULTIES: Climbing the mountain; endurance; altitude; shortness of breath.

PREPARATION: Mountain climbing school; a sense of adventure helps.

COST: Climbing gear; maybe special hiking or high-altitude insurance.

PLEASURE: Rapid.

RISKS: Numerous: slipping, hypothermia, altitude sickness.

INCONVENIENCES: The snow that falls into your briefs when you try to get dressed in a hurry.

skiing in quebec

"One fine day while out skiing in the sunlight, we found ourselves alone in nature. Everything was pure white, a real fairy tale of pleasures. Lying on our skis, we could hear others swishing by. The fear of getting caught fueled our excitement. It felt like there was magic in the air. I had the distinct pleasure of doing something that most people never get the chance to do. I allowed myself this extravagance, a romp outside of the designated conjugal bed." — Sarah, on canoe.qc

When it starts to get cold, it is time to go inside.